BLIST
AND
BLISS

A TREKKER'S GUIDE
TO THE
WEST COAST TRAIL

BY
DAVID FOSTER AND WAYNE AITKEN
ILLUSTRATED BY NELSON DEWEY

Published by:
B & B Publishing, 4081 San Capri Terrace, Victoria, B.C.,Canada, V8N 2J5
in association with:
Heritage House Publishing Company Ltd.; heritagehouse.ca

First edition: 1989
Second (revised) edition: 1991
Third (revised) edition:1995
Fourth (revised) edition: 1998
Fifth (revised) edition: 2003, 2007
Sixth (revised) edition: 2010
Seventh (revised) edition: 2014

Library and Archives Canada Cataloguing in Publication
Foster, David, 1942-, author
    Blisters and bliss: a trekker's guide to the West Coast Trail/ David Foster and Wayne Aitken; illustrated by Nelson Dewey, -- Seventh edition

Revision of: Blisters and bliss: a trekker's guide to the West Coast Trail/ by David
        Foster and Wayne Aitken ; illustrated by Nelson Dewey. --6th (rev.) ed.
        Victoria, B.C.: B&B Pub.; Surrey, B.C. : Heritage House, c2010
ISBN 978-1-927527-92-4 (pbk.)

        1. Hiking-British Columbia-West Coast Trail-Guidebooks 2.West Coast Trail (BC) - Guidebooks. I. Aitken, Wayne, 1946 - II. Dewey, Nelson III. Title.

GV199.44.C22V346 2013   796.5109711'2   C2013-908431-2

Printed in Canada, Friesens Corporation, Altona, Manitoba

ACKNOWLEDGMENTS
The West Coast Trail is a world-class trekking experience made all the more enjoyable by the contributions of the people who are continuously a part of it. We salute the lightstation keepers at Pachena and Carmanah Points, the ferry operators at Nitinat Narrows and Port Renfrew, Monique and Peter Knighton, and the maintenance workers who perform their magic every season. A tip of the old backpack goes to all the folks at Parks Canada, particularly those at the Information Centres who keep us organized and oriented. Special thanks go to the the excellent carpenters, the constantly watching Coast Guard and all the members of the First Nation bands along the way who are ready to help when we need it.

This book is dedicated to our wives, Joan and Minna, who for years have tolerated our annual treks, smoky equipment and repetitious telling of our tales. We must be doing something right during the off-season.

-David and Wayne

"Wayne who?"

-Minna Aitken, watching the home fires after
Wayne's twenty-fifth lucky hike along the Trail.

"It might take 24 hours or a week to hike the West Coast Trail, however, you need to know that after five days, I stop watering the garden at home."

-Joan Foster, watching the home fires after
Dave's twentieth lucky hike along the Trail.

A STORY

For years we have been extolling the great (and often hidden) work of Parks Canada and Coast Guard personnel. In August 2010, while researching the 6th. Edition, their contribution toward safe treks became personal. After 36 years of hiking the trail, Dave's knee finally gave out at Carmanah Creek. As luck would have it, we knew the Parks Canada's WCT Rescue Crew were at the Light Station. Wayne hiked to the Station and reported our predicament. Within minutes, Public Safety and Resource Management Specialists, Sibylla Helms and Shannon Dixon, with the assistance of Jerry Etzkorn, the lighthouse keeper, were mobilized to help us. Sibylla and Shannon hiked to Carmanah Creek, examined Dave and carried his pack back to the Carmanah Point for our medical evacuation. Two Zodiak rides later, one involving rowing through acres of bull kelp and the other, a thrilling one and a half hour blast through four foot chop, we arrived in Port Renfrew wet and cold but safe, sound and immensely grateful. We acknowledge the highly professional work performed by these folks and are grateful they are part of the trail and are our friends. Other current members of the West Coast Trail Crew, who are involved in about 70 medical evacuations a year, are Geoff Carrow, Danielle Thompson and the intrepid Rick Holmes. Thank you all.

Dave and Wayne

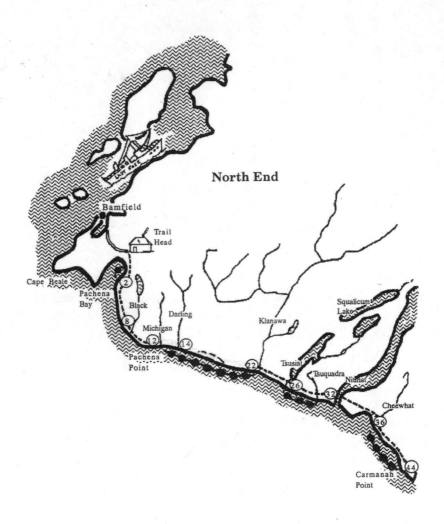

North End

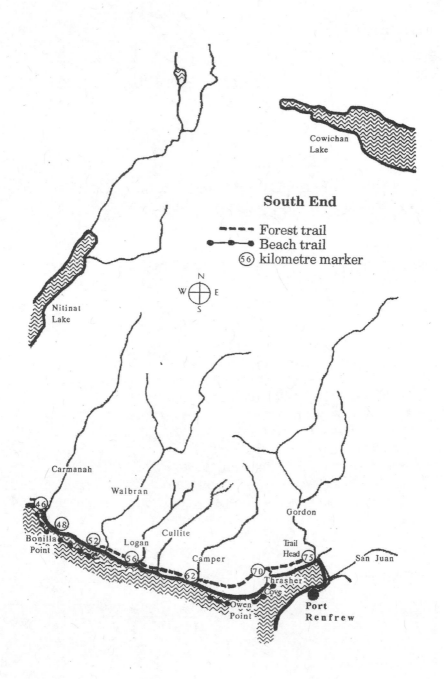

CONTENTS

TREKKING NORTH TO SOUTH 19

TREKKING SOUTH TO NORTH 94

INTRODUCTION

Each year thousands of trekkers tackle the 75 km West Coast Trail on Vancouver Island between Pachena Bay near Bamfield and Port Renfrew. Of these, hundreds come from other countries, many are repeat performers and no one forgets the experience.

Hiking the West Coast Trail, as with any world-class trek, can be a time of immense pleasure or exhausting agony. The difference is usually in the amount of care taken in planning and preparing for the trip.

Volumes have been written on backpacking techniques, so we do not intend this to be another "How To" digest. Nor do we want to explain what you will find around every corner, mud hole or ladder. We leave that magic for you to discover. Instead, we have tried to give you a sensible overview of the key areas of interest, trouble spots and distances.

We hope *Blisters and Bliss* will make your adventure safer and more enjoyable. We would love to hear your comments.
Our email address is *wtaitken@shaw.ca*. You can also find us on our website at *http://www.blistersbliss.ca/*

For simplicity, we have referred to the Bamfield end as the "North" and the Port Renfrew end as the "South". In this 7th edition, we have written the guide in two sections to accommodate the needs of both North and South-bound trekkers. We have included a number of tips for novices and trail masters alike. They are to support our main goal of providing a safe and practical guide to the West Coast Trail.

Be aware that the Parks Canada map does not take into consideration the many dips and climbs along the way. It will seem like some KM markers are much farther apart than others. It's because they are if you include the declines and inclines. Instead of just focusing on the markers to guide your day, refer as well to the approximate hiking times we have suggested at the beginning of each chapter. They will give you a more realistic sense of the actual distance your boots will be carrying you.

If you pack a lot of common sense along with your moleskin and trail mix, you will have a wonderful time. When you see us along the way, stop around for some cowboy coffee, and tell us your story.
- DAVID FOSTER and WAYNE AITKEN

HISTORY OF THE TRAIL

Construction of what is now known as the West Coast Trail began in 1889. It was originally part of an international communication system called the "Red Route." The system connected the British Empire in North America by an undersea cable which ran from Bamfield to India, via Suva in Fiji.

A part of this telegraph network ran down the west coast of Vancouver Island. It connected light stations at Cape Beale and Carmanah Point with other light stations and towns toward Victoria. The original trail, therefore, was constructed by telegraph linesmen who strung and maintained lines.

The communication route ran past the museum in Sooke where you can still see part of the original line.

The region was christened "Graveyard of the Pacific" for good reason. Over fifty ships have gone to rest here during the past one hundred years —nearly one per kilometre. Bits and pieces of many of these ships remain strewn along the coast. The huge boiler of the *Michigan*, that went down in 1893 at Michigan Creek, is still visible at low tide. Anchors, capstans, overturned hulls and unrecognizable "things" from other ships are also common.

"...unrecognizable 'things'..."

On January 22, 1906, the passenger ship *S.S. Valencia* went down on a rocky reef approximately 9 km south of Pachena Point. One hundred and twenty six passengers and crew perished with her.

The trail was substantially improved in 1907 to assist survivors of the many shipwrecks which have occurred along this rugged shore. It then became known as the "Life Saving Trail." From 1907 to 1912 workers cleared the trail and widened it to four metres between Bamfield and Pachena Point. The rugged terrain made the 4 metre width impractical to build between Pachena and Carmanah Point, so the width was reduced to 1.5 metres over this section. The primitive telegraph trail continued beyond Carmanah to Port Renfrew.

Evidence of some of the equipment that was used to either clear the trail or assist in bygone logging operations still exists. Look for an old "donkey" steam engine and grader between Billygoat and Trestle creeks. A larger engine and several metres of stretched cable are easily noticed on the trail between Thrasher Cove and Gordon River.

Modern technology, such as radio telephones and helicopters made the Life Saving Trail obsolete. Maintenance on the trail stopped in 1954, except between Pachena Point and Bamfield. Salal, salmon berry and branching evergreens soon invaded.

In l969, with plans to include this region in the third phase of the development of the Pacific Rim National Park, Canadian Parks Service sent in several crews to re-open the trail. Conservationists and logging companies went head-to-head in a campaign to have their interests protected. Today we have a world class hiking trail. Pacific Rim National Park Reserve was formally proclaimed on February 19, 2001.

The trail has improved greatly since the early 1970's when ladders were scarce and bridges an endangered species. Funding cuts, weather and heavy usage have taken their toll on today's trail. Boardwalks have deteriorated in many locations and ladder rungs may not be stable. Be aware and use great caution in these areas.

WHO ARE THE TREKKERS?

Today, thousands of people use the trail. For those who get off on statistics here are a few for your files. There were 5600 hikers in 2013. Canadians accounted for 84% of them. American interest was strong at 10% and overseas folks accounted for a further 6%. The remainder were in witness protection programs. The proportion of male to female trekkers was 53% to 47%. The average group size is 3.1 people. (The few .1 people that we have met along the trail have been very pleasant, but a little weary from trying to climb over the mushroom caps.)

The West Coast Trail is a "dog-free zone." Leave Fido at home to guard your place, while you enjoy a do-do-free trek in one of the best hiking areas in the world.

QUOTA SYSTEM

Parks Canada uses a quota and reservation system to reduce impact on the trail and park resources. While an unrestricted number of hikers can access the trail during the "shoulder seasons" (May 1 to June 14 and September 16 to September 30), limits have been established for the peak season (June 15 to September 15). A maximum of 60 may start each day: 30 hikers from the North and 30 from the South. 25 spaces are for trekkers who reserve and 5 are for hikers who are on standby.

RESERVATION SYSTEM

Reservations, while not essential, are highly recommended. Reservations are neither required nor provided during the shoulder seasons (May 1 to June 14 and September 16 to September 30). There are no quotas on week days during the shoulder seasons, so if you show up, you trek!

Beginning 8:00 am (PST) on April 17, reservations can be made online for any date between June 15 and September 15, through the Parks Canada Reservation Service. Spaces fill quickly so consider setting up an account before April 17. Go to *www.pc.gc.ca/pacificrim* and follow the link for *WCT Reservations*. You can also reserve by telephone through their call centre, 8am to 6pm (PST), seven days a week.

Canada/USA:
1-800-737-3783
or **International:**
250-726-4453

Cost of reservation in 2014 was $24.50 per person, plus Park User and Ferry fees. (see below)

PARK USER AND FERRY FEES

Every hiker must pay a park user fee, plus a ferry fee. The user fee is currently (2014) $127.50 Cdn per person while the ferry fee is $32.00 per person. Both are payable when you register at one of the trailhead information centres if you did not make a reservation. You will be issued an **Overnight Use Permit**, which must be carried with you throughout the trek. It must be turned back in to the information centre at the end of the trail. Ferry operators will check it before taking you on board, so *carry your permit in a safe, accessible place.*

ORIENTATION SESSIONS

All registered trekkers must participate in an orientation session conducted by Parks Canada staff at one of the trailhead information centres. Presentations include information on safety, environmental impact, trail conditions and history. Tide tables are also provided. Orientation sessions are presented at 9:30 a.m., 1:30 p.m. and 3:30 p.m. at both trailheads. The Gordon River Information Centre also provides a session at noon. Hikers trying to get an early start may attend the 3:30 orientation session held the day before. The registration and orientation processes take about 1 1/2 hours.

Further information can be obtained from Parks Canada, 250-726-3500.

A WORD TO THE WISE

The Parks Canada service staff have provided tremendous assistance in completing this book. They offer the following comments:

"The West Coast Trail once had the reputation of being one of the most gruelling treks in North America and as such it attracted rugged and experienced individuals. In recent years, with its reputation seemingly forgotten, the West Coast Trail has seen a tremendous increase in hiker use. Not surprisingly, each year brings numerous injuries that might have been prevented. Remember that, despite trail improvements, once you step off the boardwalk, the West Coast Trail is the same trek that it used to be. It is an isolated, prolonged and strenuous trek, that is physically challenging and potentially hazardous."

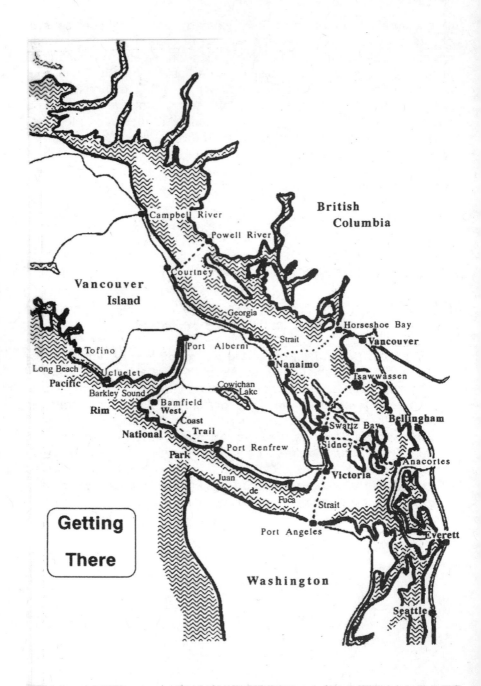

GETTING THERE

Vancouver Islanders frequently bemoan the hassles they endure getting to and from the mainland. Visiting trekkers should be prepared for this. Victoria has an international airport for those flying to the Island. The most popular means, however, is to arrive by boat.

OKAY... WE'LL PUT YOU ASHORE HERE... AND PICK YOU UP IN TEN DAYS AT PORT RENFREW...

"...the most popular means is by boat..."

B.C. Ferries operates year-round passenger services from Tsawwassen, near the south end of Vancouver, to Swartz Bay, near Victoria. Another important route carries passengers from Horseshoe Bay, north of Vancouver, to Nanaimo, near the mid-point of Vancouver Island. Nanaimo is closer to the Bamfield end of the trail. B.C. ferries leave on the odd hours from 7:00 a.m. to 9:00 p.m. throughout the year. During the busy period, from late June to early September, they run hourly. The trip, which takes approximately one and a half hours, will give you plenty of time to enjoy a bowl of clam chowder and marvel over the spectacular scenery.

The *Victoria Clipper* sails twice daily between Seattle, Washington and Victoria. The *Coho* ferry brings passengers from Port Angeles, Washington, twice daily. Washington State Ferries operates between Anacortes and Sidney (near Swartz Bay).

Getting to the trailhead from the outside world used to present all sorts of challenges. Today, there is a dependable bus service that will take you there.

The West Coast Trail Express links Victoria to Port Renfrew and Bamfield. The service runs on odd days during the WCT shoulder season and daily from June 15 to September 15. The bus leaves Victoria from in front of Pacific Coach Lines Bus Terminal, located at 700 Douglas Street, at 6:15 am. Return trips leave Bamfield at 12:45 am and Port Renfrew at 5:00 pm. The Port Renfrew trip takes about two and one half hours, while the Bamfield -Victoria run is at least a four hour adventure, half on dusty, logging roads. Complete information is posted on the West Coast Trail Express website: *www.trailbus.com*. *Phone numbers for this and other travel connections are included at the back of this book.*

TOILETS

Currently, the busiest campsites boast clean, inviting composting toilets. These works of art provide a perfect place to catch up on the next chapter of *Blisters and Bliss*. Great as they are, these conveniences will seem few and far between. Please use the toilets only for the purpose they were intended.

If there are no toilets nearby when nature calls, try to do your business below the tide line. We call it "surfing." Find a private place, dig a hole, away you go, cover it up and let the Pacific Ocean do the rest. Stay away from freshwater sources!

PUBLIC PARKING

There are a number of locations near the trailheads where vehicles can be left. Contact the information centre at your trailhead for current details (Pachena Bay: 250-728-3234; Gordon River: 250-647-5434).

TIPS BEFORE YOU BEGIN

• *Carry tide tables and a watch.   Leave yourself plenty of time to trek beach areas where tide levels make a difference.*

"...use biodegradable soap.."

• *Use biodegradable soap products to give nature and other trekkers a break.*

• *Scrub your pots and pans with sand and ocean water. It is abundant, cheap, effective, and will not pollute.*

• *Pack the heaviest items high and close to your back. This will keep the centre of gravity as normal as possible and improve your balance.*

• *Extra boot laces take little room and can serve as a clothesline, pack/ tent repair kit, bedroll straps, etc. Who knows, you might even need them to tie up your boots!*

• *Pack each meal in a separate plastic bag, then pack each day's meals in a common bag and label it. This method provides quick access to your food and reduces the chances of breakage due to handling.*

• *Leave glass containers at home. They are heavy, fragile and a source of pollution.*

• *Bring a pair of running shoes or sandals to wear around the campsite. The comfort they bring is worth their weight in treasury bills.*

• *Bring along a bladder from a wine or apple-juice box. You can keep several litres of water at your campsite and it collapses into a handful when you pack up.*

• *Pack stoves and fuel in plastic bags to keep spills and fumes contained. Stoves often have nasty edges, so cover them well.*

• *Prepare to treat all drinking water by filtering, boiling or iodine.*

Early Trekker
This illustration was first printed in the West Coast Trail Information Centre's Report, 1972.

NOTE:
TREKKING SOUTH TO NORTH begins on page 94.

TREKKING NORTH TO SOUTH

Hikers starting from the north end may reach Bamfield by vehicle from Port Alberni, or from Victoria via the logging roads that skirt Lake Cowichan, Nitinat and beyond. There are also chartered float planes available at most towns on the Island. The road between Port Alberni and Bamfield is very rough and takes a full 2 hours to drive.

One of the most popular means of transportation is *Lady Rose Marine Services*, named after the venerable *M.V. Lady Rose*, a 1930's vintage cargo and passenger vessel that plied the Alberni Inlet for 70 years. Today you can sail on her younger sister, the *M.V. Frances Barkley* who continues delivering mail and supplies to the small coastal towns. At Bamfield, she drops off and picks up her precious load of trekkers.

The *Frances Barkley*, a 128 ft. vessel, was built in Norway in 1958. In 1990 she arrived in Port Alberni via the Panama Canal. She now transports anxious trekkers to the trail or to hot showers, depending on their destination.

The *Frances Barkley*, covers the distance between Port Alberni and Bamfield on Tuesdays, Thursdays and Saturdays. Extra sailings are added on Sundays during July and August. Reservations are recommended (see **Travel Connections** on page 142 for more details). The trip takes about 4.5 hours and is a wonderful introduction to the west coast.

The Frances Barkley currently departs from the Port Alberni quay at 8:00 am and arrives in Bamfield at 12:30 pm on Tuesdays, Thursdays and Saturdays. She leaves Bamfield at 1:30 pm and arrives in Port Alberni at 5:00 pm.

The Sunday sailing departs Port Alberni at 8:00 am and arrives in Bamfield at 1:30 pm. She leaves Bamfield 3:00 pm and arrives in Port Alberni at 6:15 pm.

Get to the dock early to watch the ship being loaded. Sample the freshly made doughnuts and coffee in the little shop nearby. For those with a heartier appetite, we recommend the Blue Door Cafe, which is located near the entrance to the quay. The food is great, the portions substantial, and the ambiance... well anyway, the service is prompt and friendly.

The trailhead is about 5 kilometres over a gravel road from the Bamfield dock. If a van is not at the dock to transport you, walk up to the general store at the end of the dock to inquire about transportation. The stretch of road can be hiked by purists in about an hour, but it is very dusty and unexciting. There is a fabulous campsite on Pachena Beach, which is located at the trailhead.

"...the road can be hiked..."

NITINAT LAKE

While there is currently no access to the trail from Nitinat Village, Parks Canada is considering changing this policy for 2015. Check their website for further details. You may now leave the trail from Nitinat Narrows. A water taxi will take you from the trail at Nitinat Narrows to the town's dock, a trip that takes about a half hour, depending on weather and availability.

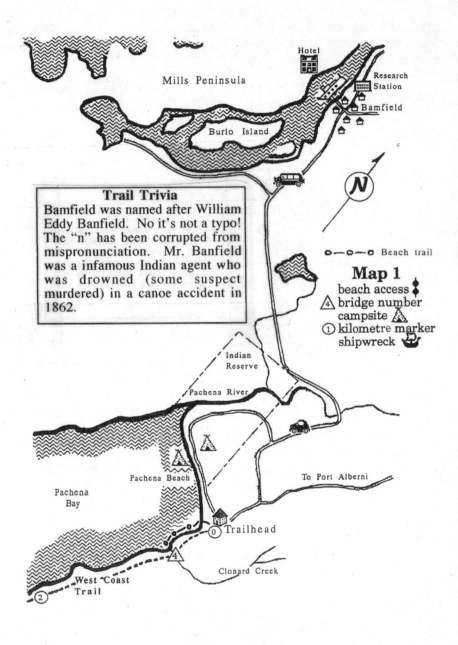

Mills Peninsula

Hotel

Research Station

Bamfield

Burlo Island

Trail Trivia
Bamfield was named after William Eddy Banfield. No it's not a typo! The "n" has been corrupted from mispronunciation. Mr. Banfield was a infamous Indian agent who was drowned (some suspect murdered) in a canoe accident in 1862.

N

O—O—O Beach trail

Map 1
beach access
bridge number
campsite
kilometre marker
shipwreck

Indian Reserve

Pachena River

Pachena Beach

To Port Alberni

Pachena Bay

Trailhead

Clonard Creek

West Coast Trail

2

MAP 1: PACHENA BAY—THE BEGINNING

Hikers must register at the Information Centre. Its operating hours are 9.00 a.m. to 5 p.m. from May 1 to September 30. A short video about the trail is shown; maps and tide tables are distributed. Current warnings are communicated (bear seen at Orange Juice Creek, cable car out at Walbran, bridge down at Sandstone, stinky trekker at Carmanah etc.) See page 13 for *Orientation*.

Now that you are at the trailhead, there is only one means of transportation left- you guessed right...

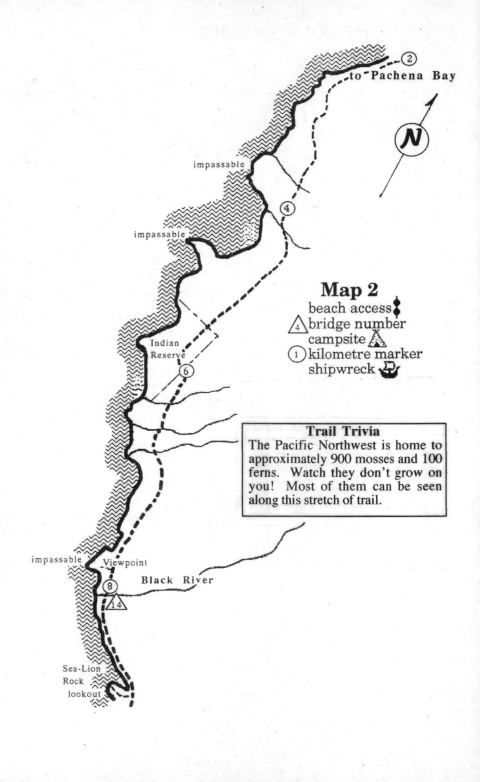

to Pachena Bay

N

impassable

impassable

Map 2
beach access
⚠ bridge number
campsite ⛺
① kilometre marker
shipwreck ⛵

Indian
Reserve

⑥

Trail Trivia
The Pacific Northwest is home to
approximately 900 mosses and 100
ferns. Watch they don't grow on
you! Most of them can be seen
along this stretch of trail.

impassable Viewpoint
⑧ **Black River**
⚠14

Sea-Lion
Rock
lookout

MAP 2: PACHENA BAY TRAILHEAD—BLACK RIVER

APPROXIMATE TREKKING TIME: 2 1/2 - 3 HOURS
DISTANCE: 8 KM

The trail is very well groomed along most of this section. It is removed from ocean views for the most part, but the woods are wonderful. This is one of the easiest sections of the entire hike and a nice warm-up for a heavy pack. Do not be lulled into thinking this is an easy stroll. It is 12 kilometres from Pachena Bay to the first campsite at Michigan Creek.

BEACH OPTION

If tides are below 2.4 metres, you can begin your hike on the beach in front of the trail head. This stroll ends at the mouth of Clonard Creek. A short side-trail brings you to the main trail near KM 1. It can save you many minutes and eliminate several long ladders.

KM 4

Just past KM 4, there is a viewpoint a few metres from the trail. We do not recommend that you go down to the beach at this point. It is too steep for safe climbing. Instead, enjoy the great views here, as well as near KM 6 and KM 8 just north of Black River.

BLACK RIVER

The Black River is crossed by bridge. The water has a high mineral content, so do not drink it. There is tap water at both Pachena Point light station and the trailhead.

Tip:
Whenever possible, lean your pack on a log before putting it on or taking it off to save wear and tear on your back.

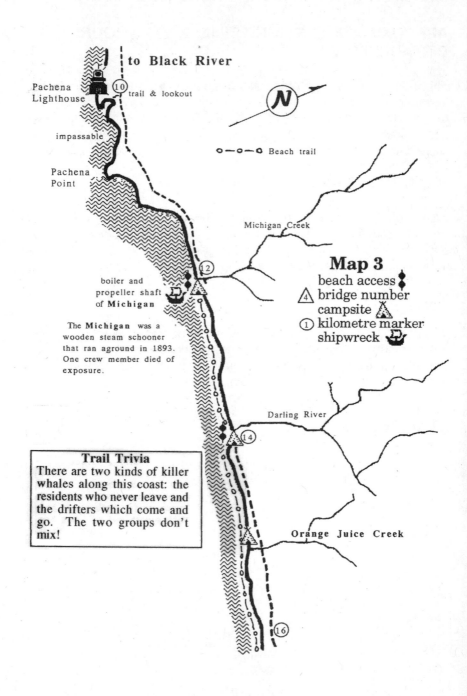

to Black River

Pachena
Lighthouse

trail & lookout

impassable

Pachena
Point

Michigan Creek

Map 3
beach access
bridge number
campsite
kilometre marker
shipwreck

boiler and
propeller shaft
of **Michigan**

The **Michigan** was a
wooden steam schooner
that ran aground in 1893.
One crew member died of
exposure.

Darling River

o—o—o Beach trail

Orange Juice Creek

Trail Trivia
There are two kinds of killer
whales along this coast: the
residents who never leave and
the drifters which come and
go. The two groups don't
mix!

MAP 3: BLACK RIVER—ORANGE JUICE CREEK

APPROXIMATE TREKKING TIME: 2-3 HOURS
DISTANCE: 7.5 KM

PACHENA POINT LIGHT STATION

Pachena Point light station is about 2 kilometres from Black River and 2 kilometres from Michigan Creek. If the grounds are open there are excellent views to enjoy.

If you are lucky, you will see gray whales "doing their thing" off the rocks at the light station. We have seen them so close to shore that the noise from their blowholes was clearly audible and their spray nearly watered the lawn!

MICHIGAN CREEK

Michigan Creek is about one hour via the trail from the light station. It has plenty of water, but firewood can be a problem late in the season. This is one of the most heavily used campsites, due to its easy access from the north and pleasant location. There are plenty of campsites on both sides of the creek. The boiler of the *Michigan,* which ran aground on the shelf in 1893, is clearly visible at low tide. This is an excellent place to admire sunsets and check out tidal pools on hot, clear days. Whales are frequently seen feeding on the shelf.

DARLING RIVER

Darling is easily reached by beach from Michigan Creek. Just follow the shore. Darling has excellent campsites with plenty of water and wood.

The ease of crossing the Darling changes from year to year and season to season. Sometimes you can tiptoe across on the stones, other times you might find a few criss-crossing logs. Most any time you can kick off your boots and enjoy the wade.

ORANGE JUICE CREEK

Orange Juice is about 1.5 kilometres from Darling and is reached only by beach. Tides must be below 2.7 metres. There is an excellent campsite here that is seldom used. Welcome to the joys and sometimes agony of beach walking!

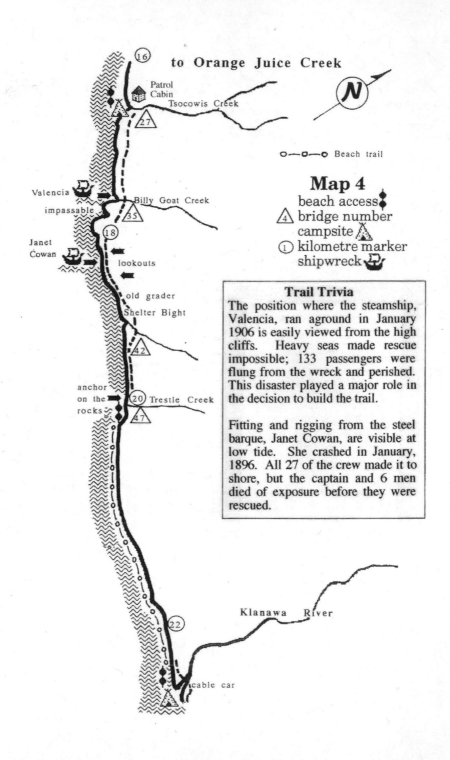

to Orange Juice Creek

16

Patrol Cabin

Tsocowis Creek

27

O—O—O Beach trail

Map 4
beach access
△4 bridge number
campsite △
①1 kilometre marker
shipwreck

Valencia

impassable

Billy Goat Creek

35

Janet Cowan

18

lookouts

old grader

Shelter Bight

42

anchor on the rocks

20 Trestle Creek

47

Trail Trivia

The position where the steamship, Valencia, ran aground in January 1906 is easily viewed from the high cliffs. Heavy seas made rescue impossible; 133 passengers were flung from the wreck and perished. This disaster played a major role in the decision to build the trail.

Fitting and rigging from the steel barque, Janet Cowan, are visible at low tide. She crashed in January, 1896. All 27 of the crew made it to shore, but the captain and 6 men died of exposure before they were rescued.

Klanawa River

22

cable car

MAP 4: ORANGE JUICE CREEK—KLANAWA RIVER

APPROXIMATE TREKKING TIME: 2 1/2 HOURS
DISTANCE: 8 KM

The terrain along this stretch varies from easy beach trekking at either end, to rugged cliffs with lookouts between Billy Goat and Trestle creeks. Even on the higher stretches, the trail is well maintained and easily hiked. Most of the terrain is flat along this section, albeit high above the water. In many places, the inland route is like a stroll to grandma's house.

TSOCOWIS CREEK

There is an excellent campsite next to a waterfall on the north side of Tsocowis. You will find plenty of firewood and water here. Steep ladders willl take you high above the beach to the top of the waterfall. A swinging bridge takes you over the creek. The view is spectacular. The lookouts between Billy Goat and Trestle creeks provide other opportuniities to shoot some frames.

An impassable headland near the south side of Billy Goat and the steep cliffs of the Valencia Bluffs are fair warning to keep to the inland trail between Tsocowis and the beach access at Trestle Creek.

VALENCIA LOOKOUT

The views from here are unique and overlook the site where the iron steamship *Valencia* went down in heavy seas in 1906. You do not want to be on the beach here under any circumstances.

Tip:
This is a popular place to drop packs and dig into your power bars and trail mix. Be careful where you sit and set your packs. The tree roots at the side of the trail are covered with pitch.

Look for the old grader on the trail near the Valencia lookout. There is also a rusted-out donkey engine close to Shelter Bight. Early trekkers used to run up and down the trail with these strapped on their backs just to keep in shape, or so the story goes.

TRESTLE CREEK

The trail rejoins the beach at Trestle Creek. This is a favourite spot for north and south-bound hikers to stop for a snack and enjoy the views. Look for the old anchor on the rocks. It may be from the steamship, Woodside, which went down near here in 1888.   You must hike the beach route from here to Klanawa, but check that the tides are below 2.7 metres before you leave.

KLANAWA RIVER

The section between Trestle Creek and Klanawa provides good beach walking, mostly via stone shelf, but with boulders thrown in for good measure.

Access to the cable car at Klanawa is best gained by the beach access, which is about 50 meters from the river on the north side. The river-edge route is a little more rugged. Branches often extend onto this path and test your good humour. There are campsites by the north side of Klanawa for those who do not wish to continue on to Tsusiat, approximately 3 kilometres to the south.

Stay on the trail between Klanawa and Tsusiat Falls. There are impassable headlands between KM 24 and the falls.

DAVE'S ADVICE ON MICE

No other creature will have such a profound affect on your hike as the innocent field mouse.

On a rare, still and sultry night on a west coast beach, we left the tent flap open just a smidgeon to make the thick, body-odoured air more tolerable. Late in the night, gentle scratchings and crunchings awakened us. A tiny moving thing scampered across my sleeping bag. Wayne yelled, "The little s.o.b. ran across my face!"

I believe I know about mice. To thwart a mouse, you must place all desirable mouse food in a sack and hang it high. If you stay in the same place two nights in a row, be wary. Your average mouse will have located your stuff the first night. Be cool; be clever; be crafty. Fool him by storing your pack and your food in a new spot the second night. I speak from experience. At Carmanah, a mouse chewed through the canvas of my pack to reach some overlooked trail mix. Trail mix, I've discovered, is very desirable mouse food.

Never underestimate the athletic ability of mice. One evening at Cribs Creek, after the food was hung, I discovered a partial bag of trail mix still in my pack. Feeling smug, I took the little baggy of nuts and lashed it to a loose rope end near the main food bag. At least six inches separated the two bags as they swung in space. The small bag was so light and unstable, it swayed in the wind. I was confident no reasonable mouse would attempt such a challenge. Wrong! The next morning the hanging baggy had a tidy hole. Only the raisins remained. We may need further study, but I suspect raisins are not desirable mouse food.

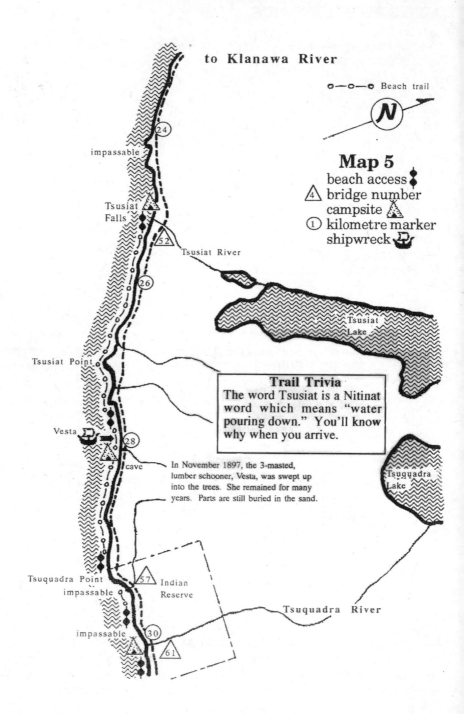

to Klanawa River

Beach trail

Map 5
beach access
△4 bridge number
campsite △
① kilometre marker
shipwreck

24

impassable

Tsusiat
Falls

52

Tsusiat River

26

Tsusiat
Lake

Tsusiat Point

Trail Trivia
The word Tsusiat is a Nitinat
word which means "water
pouring down." You'll know
why when you arrive.

Vesta

28

cave

Tsuquadra
Lake

In November 1897, the 3-masted,
lumber schooner, Vesta, was swept up
into the trees. She remained for many
years. Parts are still buried in the sand.

Tsuquadra Point
impassable

57 Indian
Reserve

Tsuquadra River

impassable

30

61

MAP 5: KLANAWA RIVER—TSUQUADRA POINT

APPROXIMATE TREKKING TIME: 2 1/2 TO 3 HOURS
DISTANCE: 7 KM

The trail from Klanawa River to Tsusiat Falls is all inland. Climb up, climb down. Impressive ladders lead you to new heights. Be extra cautious on the boardwalks between KM 24 and the falls. A slip on these can cause you grief when you least expect it. So too, can overhanging branches.

TSUSIAT FALLS

Tsusiat Falls campsite is one of the most popular campsites along the entire route. Do not take the small, unmarked trail that turns to the right immediately after crossing the river bridge. This dangerous path leads to the top of the falls. There is drop of about 20 metres to the bottom if you slip. Instead, carry on for a few more minutes until you come to the ladders leading to the beach. They are steep and high and will give you enough thrills without jumping off the waterfall. Tsusiat Falls is a spectacular natural feature that draws thousands of visitors each year. It provides a refreshing opportunity for sunbathers and dusty travellers to clean up and forget about the rigours of the walk for awhile. There are rock shelves to sit on behind the falls, but be careful—they are slippery and can be dangerous.

The outstanding beauty of this campground is constantly threatened by heavy use. Parks Canada has solved part of the problem by providing a luxurious composting toilet at the north end of the bay. Our role as users is to help keep the sand clean by containing fires and picking up after ourselves. It is no fun having to clean up someone else's mess after sweating it out in the harness all day. We really hope everyone realizes this.

The route between Tsusiat Falls and KM 29 can be covered either on the beach or via the inland trail. The trail offers periodic views of the ocean and welcome shade on blistering hot days, should you be so lucky. The beach is spectacular, but the sand is loose and can be hard slogging. Watch for some remarkable trees near KM 30.

Travel between Tsusiat Falls and Tsusiat Point is an easy beach boogie. Beach access trails are identified near the point by the usual array of coloured floats. Tsusiat Point is passable through the "hole in the wall" at tides below 2.1 metres.

Tip:
Load up on water at Tsusiat Falls. This is a long, "dry" stretch.

TSUQUADRA POINT

Beach access is located near KM 28 or at KM 29. The trail passes through an Indian Reserve near KM 30 and Tsuquadra Point. Signs are posted to restrict beach access while in this special area. Please respect their message. A bridge that used to cross a creek between Tsuquadra Point and KM 30 was destroyed in a storm. Take care crossing the rubble.

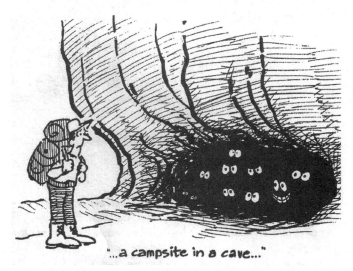

"...a campsite in a cave..."

There is a campsite in a cave along the trail, midway between Tsusiat Falls and Tsuquadra Point. The cave is approximately 100 square metres, with enough height for standing and could serve as a foul-weather shelter. Much of the trail is flat here and the trees are magnificent. It is well worth staying in the woods. The trail is much higher between KM 31 and Nitinat Narrows. The views are spectacular—even on dreary days. As you near Nitinat Narrows, the trail dips and heads inland over many boardwalks, bridges, ladders and intertwined roots.

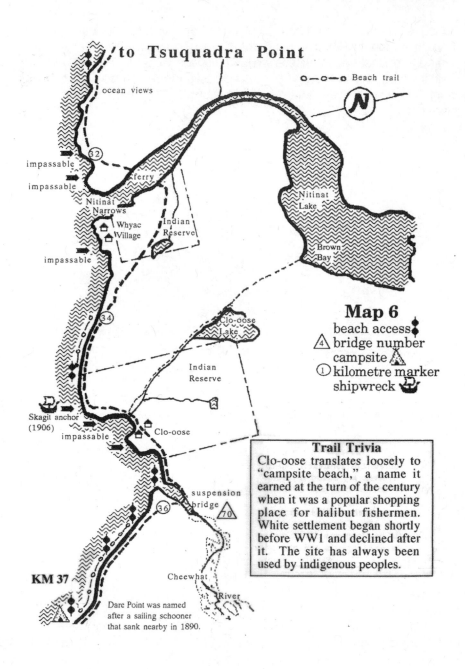

to Tsuquadra Point

ocean views

○—○—○ Beach trail

N

impassable → 62

impassable → ferry

Nitinat
Narrows

Nitinat
Lake

Whyac
Village

Indian
Reserve

Brown
Bay

impassable →

34

Clo-oose
Lake

Indian
Reserve

Map 6

beach access ⬥
△4 bridge number
campsite ⛺
① kilometre marker
shipwreck ⛵

Skagit anchor
(1906)

impassable →

Clo-oose

suspension
bridge

36 ⛺70

Trail Trivia
Clo-oose translates loosely to "campsite beach," a name it earned at the turn of the century when it was a popular shopping place for halibut fishermen. White settlement began shortly before WW1 and declined after it. The site has always been used by indigenous peoples.

KM 37

Cheewhat

River

⛺

Dare Point was named
after a sailing schooner
that sank nearby in 1890.

MAP 6: TSUQUADRA POINT—KM 37

APPROXIMATE TREKKING TIME: 3 1/2 HOURS
DISTANCE: 8 KM
(Time will vary with availability of ferry service at Nitinat Narrows)

NITINAT NARROWS

Nitinat Narrows must be crossed by boat. The current runs up to eight knots and the water is cold and deep. The water looks inviting, but it is not drinkable because of the high salt content.

There are magnificent trees growing on the north side of the Narrows and high bluffs offer spectacular views. Be careful on the boardwalk leading to the crossing point.

The ferry operator makes periodic checks for trekkers to take them the short distance across the river. If he is not visible, drop your packs, put your feet up and enjoy the scenery. There is no other option.

Carl Edgar, Jr., his family, friends and a wonderful assortment of dogs and kids take trekkers across the narrows in their open fishing boat. There may be fresh seafood available here for reasonable prices. Many a year we've cooked fresh lingcod that was so good it brought tears to our eyes! Dungeness crab is another delight to look for. Liquid treats can also be purchased. Please deposit all empty cans in the bins provided near the dock.

Timing is critical at this point since the ferry service operates between 9:00 a.m. and 5:00 p.m. May 1 to September 30. There are several crossings each day and this is also the departure point for hikers leaving the trail to go to Nitinat Village. Once again, the Nitinat Narrows are always salty. Take care to carry lots of water when you trek this section. Do not rely on getting water here.

CHEEWHAT RIVER

The trail between Nitinat and Cheewhat River is mainly inland along extensive boardwalks that cut across Indian Reserves. Excellent time can be made hiking this stretch, but please be careful if the boards are wet. We both have cedar slat imprints on our butts from slips in bygone years.

A suspension bridge spans the Cheewhat River. It is "user friendly" and sometimes provides shade for raccoons and river creatures. If you are low on water, look for a spring in the woods near the north end of the bridge. The Cheewat is fresh water, but not suitable for drinking because of its foul taste.

Beach access is located just past KM 36. While we have camped along this beach many times in the past, restrictions have recently been applied between KM 36 and KM 37 due to an abundance of wildlife in the area. Check with Parks Canada before planning to camp here.

The Cheewhat is aptly named. We have heard that one translation of Cheewhat is "River of Urine"—enough said. Hope you brought a good supply of water!

40

KM 37

The section between Cheewhat and KM 37 is one of our favourites. The woods are peaceful, the trail is very wide and level in most places, and the beach—ahhh, the beach, 1 1/2 kilometres of lovely white sand! Bathe your blisters and enjoy!

The bad news is that there is almost no water alonq the entire stretch. There is a small "stream" (read: dribble of water) that is right at KM 37 near the most southerly point of the beach. A pool may have to be dug to get enough water for cooking. Take special care to boil or treat this water before drinking.

Occasionally, vast flocks of seagulls take over this area. They can do some interesting things to the quality of drinking water in a small stream, so be prepared to move on if they have moved in before you. The Dare Point mouse brigade has claimed squatters' rights on any food that is left open. Hang your pantry high if you are staying near this gang.

Tip:
If you are staying at KM 37 and want to get water from the small stream and have trouble getting enough into your bottle, scoop a hole in the stream bed and line it with a few stones. After the silt settles it should make a fine watering hole.

Hike at a pace comfortable for the slowest trekker in your group. This will keep you in sight of each other and help ensure that everyone arrives safely with energy to spare.

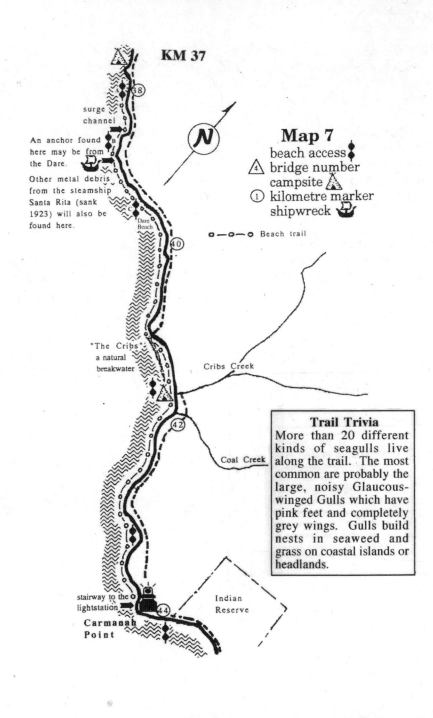

KM 37

surge channel

An anchor found here may be from the Dare.

Other metal debris from the steamship Santa Rita (sank 1923) will also be found here.

Dare Beach

"The Cribs" a natural breakwater

Cribs Creek

Coal Creek

stairway to the lightstation

Carmanah Point

Indian Reserve

Map 7
beach access
△ bridge number
campsite
① kilometre marker
shipwreck

o—o—o Beach trail

MAP 7: KM 37—CARMANAH POINT

APPROXIMATE TREKKING TIME: 2 1/2 TO 3 HOURS
DISTANCE: 6 KM

This section can be hiked by trail or, if tides are right, by beach. The trail route has interesting views, some from high vantage points.

KM 38 SURGE CHANNEL

There is a difficult surge channel just south of KM 38. For this reason, we recommend that trekkers take the trail from KM 37 until at least KM 39. (access B) Then, if the tides are right, you can scoot along to the Cribs, Coal Creek and eventually Carmanah Point. This is the preferred route. Do not take access A, this is mainly intended for north bound trekkers. The rocks in this area are very slippery. Tides must be below 2.1 metres before you tackle this section. The *Santa Rita*, which went down in 1923, left its debris along this stretch. It can do the same to you. Your safest alternative is to stay on the inland trail.

Tip:

If you insist on going on the beach between KM 39 and Dare Point, look for a grapefruit-sized rock protruding from the north face of the shelf at KM 39. This rock provides the only foothold for getting up from the beach to the shelf. An alternative is to look for a rope that may be hanging over the shelf. If it's there it will assist you with your assent.

CRIBS CREEK

Water is seasonally dependent along this route until you get to Cribs or Coal creek. There is one other campsite, at KM 40, that may have water. This is a lovely spot and seldom used.

The Cribs Creek water is better than at KM 40, but the best is at Carmanah. Remember, it may look great but it must be treated.

The "Cribs" boasts a natural, rocky breakwater and is a unique coastal feature along this stretch. It is easy to hike and the scenery is spectacular. Thousands of sea birds may be resting on these rocks and along the beach. If you walk through the flock, be prepared for a loud and spectacular show of motion. Wear a hat!

Steep cliffs between KM 37 and Cribs Creek block trail access in several places. Be sure of the tide levels and give yourself plenty of time to get through this area. Do not get caught hiking here with water lapping at your feet.

CARMANAH POINT

Most of the time throughout the year there are sea lions off Carmanah Point. You can frequently hear and smell them before you actually see them. Ahhhhhh, the west coast!

The stretch between Cribs Creek and Carmanah Point can be trekked inland, or by beach. Either way is well travelled. We prefer the beach. Carmanah Point is crossed either by trekking the regular trail and bypassing the light station or by climbing a long flight of stairs from the beach at the north end. The stairs emerge on the station grounds. Many trekkers claim that these stairs are twice as high going up as they are going down. Let your body make the call!   Our friends, Janet and Jerry Etzkorn, have carefully maintained the Carmanah Light for many years. Stop and admire their garden.   You are welcome to walk Janet's homemade labyrinth and get in touch with your inner self.

Water is available here, but you can also fill up at Carmanah Creek just 2 kilometres to the south. Another flight of stairs leads down to the fabulous beach on the south side.

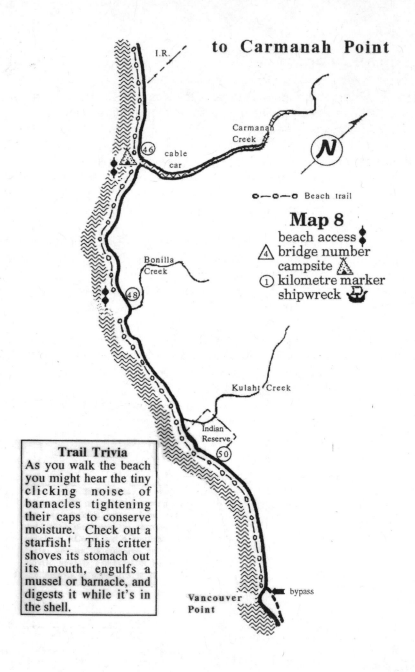

to Carmanah Point

I.R.

Carmanah
Creek

46 cable
car

o—o—o Beach trail

Map 8
beach access
△ bridge number
campsite △
① kilometre marker
shipwreck

Bonilla
Creek

48

Kulaht Creek

Indian
Reserve

50

Trail Trivia
As you walk the beach you might hear the tiny clicking noise of barnacles tightening their caps to conserve moisture. Check out a starfish! This critter shoves its stomach out its mouth, engulfs a mussel or barnacle, and digests it while it's in the shell.

bypass

Vancouver
Point

MAP 8: CARMANAH POINT—VANCOUVER POINT

APPROXIMATE TREKKING TIME: 2 1/2 TO 3 HOURS
DISTANCE: 7 KM

The beach between Carmanah Point and the campsite at Carmanah Creek is a classic. It is about 2 kilometres in length, a beautiful reward for southbounders and an easy walk.

Travel between Carmanah Point and Vancouver Point is all on the beach. There are excellent views along this sandy stretch.

Be sure to stop by Chez Monique's near the north end of the beach. Monique (if her settlement is still occupied) will tell you her story about ancient Native claims to the area. Refreshments to satisfy most cravings are available. She also has a shelter for trekkers who have run into trouble with the weather.

CARMANAH CREEK

Carmanah Creek can be waded near its mouth during July, August and September. Be careful of the strong current. If you are determined to keep dry, use the cable car. Do not go searching up and down the creek (it is more like a river than a creek) looking for a dry crossing, for they are rare. Park your pack, doff your boots and stroll across near the mouth. Your tootsies will thank you.

Carmanah Creek offers an excellent campsite with plenty of wood, fresh water and postcard-calibre views. There is an ancient horn at the Carmanah Point Light Station that no longer blows. It once had the

longest series of warning blasts along the coast—three honks every ninety seconds! It could bring tears to the eyes of weary trekkers who had just tucked in at the end of a long day. Modern technology has rendered the horn obsolete. Today we look forward to the soothing, steady roar of the surf.

CARMANAH VALLEY TREES

Carmanah Valley is the home of many of the world's tallest Sitka spruce. Some of these giants are over 3 metres in diameter and are estimated to be more than 700 years old. The tallest tree is nearly 32 stories high. We tip our packs to the Heritage Forest Society, Sierra Club and Western Canada Wilderness Committee for their unfaltering efforts to save these treasures from chainsaws.

...fine sand makes for tough trekking...

BONILLA POINT

Bonilla has a good campsite with plenty of wood and a small waterfall. Your only option is to hike the beach here, but it is often very tough slogging on fine sand or gravel, as you sink with every step.This is one stretch where gaiters or spats are handy for keeping the pebbles on the beach and out of your boots. Wayne likes to use the "sand-in-the-boots" trick as an excuse to stop. He takes off his boots, shakes out his socks and enjoys the scenery. It drives Dave crazy!

Passage from Bonilla to Vancouver Point is possible when tides are below 3.0 metres. There are pieces of long-lost ships stuck here and there in the sand. We have seen several river otters around here. One year we watched a dozen seals herd a school of small fish into the shallows at Kulaht as a prelude to a seafood buffet. Deer occasionally wander by. One actually allowed itself to be scratched behind its ears, just like some trekkers!

VANCOUVER POINT

Look for beach access on the north side of Vancouver Point. This trail section will end at the cable car on Walbran Creek about 2 kilometres away.

You may beach boogie between Vancouver Point and Walbran Creek if tides are below 2.7 metres and Walbran is not in flood. We recommend this route.

"...the beach boogie..."

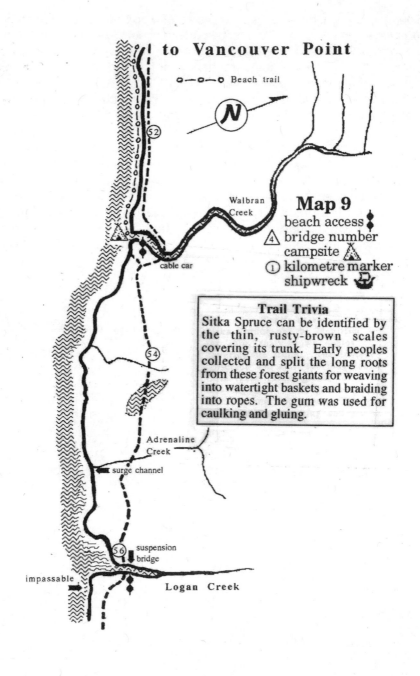

to Vancouver Point

○—○—○ Beach trail

N

Walbran
Creek

cable car

Map 9
beach access
△₄ bridge number
campsite △
①　kilometre marker
shipwreck

Trail Trivia
Sitka Spruce can be identified by
the thin, rusty-brown scales
covering its trunk. Early peoples
collected and split the long roots
from these forest giants for weaving
into watertight baskets and braiding
into ropes. The gum was used for
caulking and gluing.

Adrenaline
Creek

surge channel

suspension
bridge

impassable

Logan Creek

MAP 9: VANCOUVER POINT—LOGAN CREEK

APPROXIMATE TREKKING TIME: 2 1/2 to 3 hours
DISTANCE: 5 KM

This section has it all: steep ladders, endless mud holes and roots, boardwalks over bog, a dangerous surge channel, a cable car, a wonderful sandy beach, a fabulous swimming hole, a spectacular campsite, and a heart-thumping bridge over Logan Creek. What a trek!

WALBRAN CREEK

The stretch between Vancouver Point and Walbran Creek is passable when tides are below 2.7 metres. There is an overland route from Vancouver Point to a cable car that crosses Walbran Creek, but we recommend the beach route and then fording the creek at its mouth. If wading doesn't appeal then you must find the trail nearby that leads to the cable car. Don't try to reach the cable car by following the riverbank because it was blocked by a slide in 2011.

Walbran Creek campsite is one of the best on the trail. A clear, deep and refreshingly cool (read ice cold) pond greets weary trekkers. There is plenty of wood for fires and wind shelters.

The route between Walbran and Logan begins with a high set of ladders. It crosses a swampy area via a series of boardwalks. There are long sections where you are scampering over roots and around mud holes.

This ain't no shoppin' mall!

The bog area has some interesting plants, trees and moss. We recommend it for the nature lover and safe trekker alike. Please stay on the boardwalk along this section to preserve the fragile environment and prevent wet feet.

Tip:

Hiking poles can greatly improve your balance and help check suspicious planks on the boardwalk before you turn "turtle".

LOGAN CREEK

Recent weather events and landslides have destroyed the campsites that were once located at the mouth of the creek. There is no longer safe access to the creek from either end of the trail. Do not plan on camping here.

The Logan Creek suspension bridge is a masterpiece of engineering. It offers spectacular, if not heart-stopping, views from its centre. This is the second bridge built over this creek. The first disappeared a few years ago during a major landslide, as did the ladders accessing the beach.
The walls of the creek basin are very steep. Extensive erosion has a nasty habit of knocking trees over the ladders and around the bridge heads. As a result, the trail is often hazardous, and the ladders are in less than perfect condition. Watch each step carefully through here.

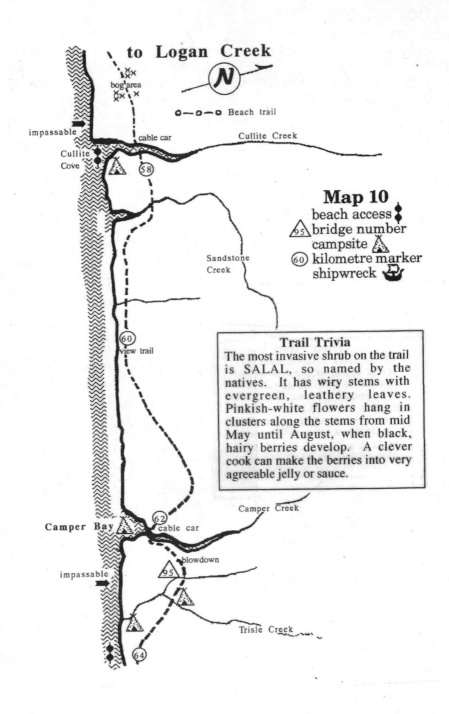

to Logan Creek

N

bog area

o—o—o Beach trail

impassable

cable car

Cullite Creek

Cullite
Cove

58

Map 10
beach access
95 bridge number
campsite
60 kilometre marker
shipwreck

Sandstone
Creek

60
view trail

Trail Trivia
The most invasive shrub on the trail
is SALAL, so named by the
natives. It has wiry stems with
evergreen, leathery leaves.
Pinkish-white flowers hang in
clusters along the stems from mid
May until August, when black,
hairy berries develop. A clever
cook can make the berries into very
agreeable jelly or sauce.

Camper Creek

Camper Bay

62
cable car

blowdown

impassable

95

Trisle Creek

64

MAP 10: LOGAN CREEK—CAMPER BAY

APPROXIMATE TREKKING TIME: 4 HOURS
DISTANCE: 6 KM   (BUT CAN SEEM LIKE DAYS)

LADDERS

They're HEEEEERE! This section includes some of the most challenging, frustrating, muddy and generally interesting terrain along the entire trail. It also has ladders—lots of ladders. Ladders with over 200 rungs (count them) which never seem to end. We are talking ladders that climb the equivalent of a 25 to 30 story building. Say hello to your cardiovascular system!

"...ladders that seem to never end..."

Tip:
Carry a walking stick along this stretch to help you keep your balance as you prance around the mud holes.

This section requires particular attention. Even if it is not raining, the trail can become a quagmire in places, so step with care and be prepared for frequent mud baths. It's great! There's enough mud and goo in this area to coat us all. In a split second you can end up knee deep or more in the stuff. Should you take the plunge, remind yourself that the world's best spas charge big bucks for this sort of skin treatment.

The trail from Logan, which has steep ladders at either end of the bridge, moves through a swampy area with boardwalks and interesting flora. Many of the trees are ancient and stunted "bonsai" cousins of giant cedars, spruce and hemlock.

CULLITE CREEK

Big ladders greet you at the cable car on Cullite Creek. If you are coming from either direction, you already know what to expect. Sandstone and Logan creeks both have their fair share of ladders, but those at Cullite are the highest of all.

There is a campsite at Cullite Cove, which is bordered by impassable headlands. You have to go down into the creek bed to get to it.

Get your cameras out—the folks back at the office are not going to believe this part of your story.

SANDSTONE CREEK

At Sandstone, as with Cullite, the ladders seem unending, particularly if you are going up. A bridge across this beautiful creek offers a welcome respite before tackling the ladders on the other side. Once you complete this section of the trail, there will be no beanstalk you cannot scale.

The trail between Sandstone and Camper Bay is a maze of giant roots, mini-bogs and fallen logs. It is easiest near the south end, but drops sharply at Camper.

Tip:
If there are no bear boxes available, be smarter than the average bear. Hang your food high and well away from your campsite.

CAMPER BAY

Camper Bay offers excellent, well-protected campsites. There is usually plenty of firewood at the head of the bay, but you may have do some fancy stone-stepping to cross the creek. The creek bed at Camper changes its course every year and sometimes disappears under the gravel before reaching the ocean.

Be wary of the tides when you pitch your tent. The creek bed may look innocent, but it floods with the rising tide.   We have heard wild blasphemy from trekkers who had snuggled down for the night only to find themselves deep in the brine before their time. Look for the high-tide line and stay above it.

Tips:
When the tide is rising, go well upstream to get fresh drinking water.
Pitch your tent at the southern end to collect sunlight a little longer.

Conceived over a period of several days, the F-K A/T HIKING BOOT is the result of numerous long (and to nearby hikers and campers, quite boring) discussions between two outdoors enthusiasts who should have been watching where they were walking (two words: deer do do).

Designed specifically with the West Coast Trail trekker in mind, this boot has many unique features, including the convertible toe cover (to allow all-over tanning), the toe-grip suction-cup insole, the built-in GPS satellite receiver, the "No-Blistr"™ cutaways at sensitive locations, and the "Beach Boogie"™ traction devices on either side of the heel. It's expected these two creative minds will be getting together on the trail again next year and designing yet another piece of footwear, which—in combination with this—will constitute a complete pair of hiking boots.

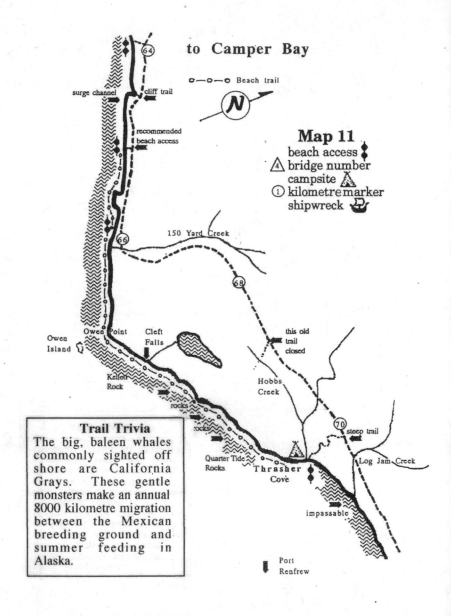

to Camper Bay

o—o—o Beach trail

N

Map 11
beach access
△ bridge number
campsite △
① kilometre marker
shipwreck

64

surge channel   cliff trail

recommended
beach access

66   150 Yard Creek

68

Owen Point   Cleft
Falls
Owen
Island
this old
trail
closed

Kellett
Rock
Hobbs
Creek

rocks

70   steep trail

rocks

Quarter Tide   Log Jam Creek
Rocks
Thrasher
Cove

impassable

Port
Renfrew

Trail Trivia
The big, baleen whales commonly sighted off shore are California Grays. These gentle monsters make an annual 8000 kilometre migration between the Mexican breeding ground and summer feeding in Alaska.

MAP 11: CAMPER BAY—THRASHER COVE

APPROXIMATE TREKKING TIME: 4 HOURS
DISTANCE: 8 KM

You must take the inland trail between Camper Bay and KM 65. Steep ladders greet you on the south side of Camper Creek, but by now you are at expert at breaching these inclines. You can take the beach or the inland trail from KM 65 to Thrasher, tides willing. Another option is to continue along the trail until KM 66 and then decide whether to take the trail or hike the beach.

The beach section offers a variety of hiking terrain, but is more challenging than the inland route. The inland trail is hidden from the ocean for most of the time. It cuts deep into the woods around Owen Point and is a marvelous forest walk. Be very careful crossing the many logs along this stretch.

SURGE CHANNEL

There is a dangerous surge channel between KM 64 and KM 65 that can be crossed when tides are below 1.7 meters but it could ruin your day if you hit it at the wrong time and need to backtrack. If the tide is low enough, a rock will be exposed in the middle of the channel. If necessary, remove your packs and pass them across one at a time. This may not be an easy process, but it may save injury.

KM 65

Beach access is available at KM 65 and 66. Both access points open onto a spectacular shelf that spans the entire section from KM 65 to Owen Point. The route is passable if tides are below 2.4 metres; however, note that Owen Point may only be rounded when tide levels are below 1.8 metres.

We strongly urge you to take the access trail at KM 65 because of its relative safety. The shelf south of KM 65 provides an excellent trekking highway. Be careful of lesser surge channels, sandstone caves and other natural barriers found along the way.

OWEN POINT

There is a spectacular cave that you must walk through to get around Owen Point provided the tide is below 1.8 metres. If the tide is rising and you find yourself at Owen Point, you may be able to climb over the point, rather than taking the cave route. Look for the ropes at either side but don't count on them being there.

Watch for the sea lions off Owen Point. They can help kill some time if the tides hold you up.

It is important to check tide tables any time you hike the beaches, but it is particularly important for this stretch. The tides must be lower than 2.4 metres to get from KM 65 to Thrasher Cove, but remember that they must be below 1.8 metres to get around Owen Point.

The lower the tide, the easier will be the hike from Owen Point to Thrasher. The beach is littered with huge crisscrossing logs and enormous boulders. This route may frequently seem impassable, but if the tides are right, and you watch your step, it is a great route to take.

The inland passage is also an interesting but challenging hike. Unfortunately, there are no ocean views for the entire distance from Camper Bay to Thrasher.

THRASHER COVE

Thrasher Cove is always a welcome sight. There are several good campsites, fresh water and usually lots of firewood. Be aware that if you arrive from the trail you will have added an extra kilometre of tricky, arduous hiking to your trek. There are a series of very steep switchbacks to maneuver and finally a set of ladders that drop you fifty stories to the beach. The climb back up makes for a tough start first thing in the morning.

Tip:
A seldom used, but reasonable alternative to going down to the beach at Thrasher, is a campsite near KM 70, about 300 metres south of the Thrasher turn off. There is room for at least two tents and water at Log Jam Creek is a few metres beyond.

63

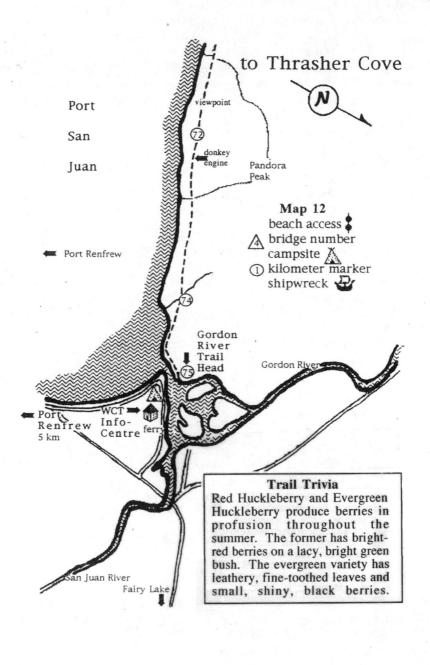

to Thrasher Cove

N

Port

San

Juan

viewpoint

72

donkey
engine

Pandora
Peak

Port Renfrew

Map 12
beach access
△4 bridge number
campsite △
① kilometer marker
shipwreck

74

Gordon
River
Trail
Head

Gordon River

75

Port
Renfrew
5 km

WCT
Info-
Centre

ferry

San Juan River

Fairy Lake

Trail Trivia
Red Huckleberry and Evergreen
Huckleberry produce berries in
profusion throughout the
summer. The former has bright-
red berries on a lacy, bright green
bush. The evergreen variety has
leathery, fine-toothed leaves and
small, shiny, black berries.

MAP 12: THRASHER COVE—GORDON RIVER

APPROXIMATE TREKKING TIME: 3 1/2 - 4 1/2 HOURS
DISTANCE: 6 KM

This section is all inland. The climb from the beach to the trail is about one kilometre of very steep ladders and switchbacks. It is often not well maintained so be prepared for some rough patches. Take your time.

The main trail is very similar to the section between KM 65 and the Thrasher turnoff. Visibility is limited, but, on clear days you may catch glimpses of Port San Juan and beyond. The highest point of the entire trail is along here. There are some lovely valleys, as well as tricky ravine crossings and rock scrambling areas. Ladders abound.

A huge, old donkey engine sits by the trail near KM 72. We have often wondered at the effort it must have taken for the early loggers to get that machine up there. Hundreds of metres of heavy cable, used decades ago to haul logs to the water, are still stretched taut along the trail.

GORDON RIVER TRAILHEAD

Congratulations! You have the trek of a lifetime behind you now, and we hope it was as much fun for you as it has been for us. Let's talk about it sometime over cowboy coffee at Carmanah. We would love hear about your adventures. Email us at *wtaitken@shaw.ca.* or *davefoster@shaw.ca*

Raise the red ball to alert the ferry operator. He makes several pickups each day. Make sure you sign out at the Parks Canada Information Centre located near the ferry dock.

INTRODUCING THE NEWEST IDEA IN "MINI-MOTORHOMES"

WALKABAGO

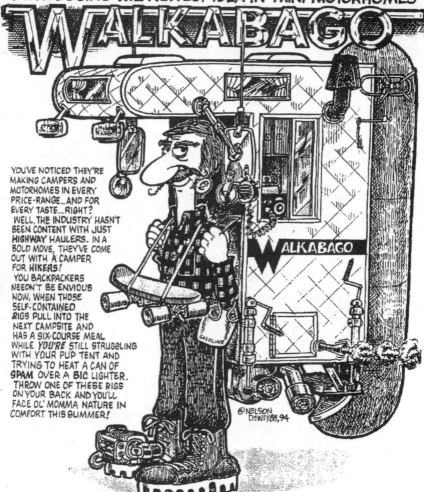

YOU'VE NOTICED THEY'RE MAKING CAMPERS AND MOTORHOMES IN EVERY PRICE-RANGE...AND FOR EVERY TASTE...RIGHT? WELL, THE INDUSTRY HASN'T BEEN CONTENT WITH JUST HIGHWAY HAULERS. IN A BOLD MOVE, THEY'VE COME OUT WITH A CAMPER FOR HIKERS! YOU BACKPACKERS NEEDN'T BE ENVIOUS NOW, WHEN THOSE SELF-CONTAINED RIGS PULL INTO THE NEXT CAMPSITE AND HAS A SIX-COURSE MEAL WHILE *YOU'RE* STILL STRUGGLING WITH YOUR PUP TENT AND TRYING TO HEAT A CAN OF *SPAM* OVER A *BIC* LIGHTER. THROW ONE OF THESE RIGS ON YOUR BACK AND YOU'LL FACE OL' MOMMA NATURE IN COMFORT THIS SUMMER!

© NELSON DEWEY '88, '94

SOME OF WALKABAGO'S FEATURES....

This rig has all the goodies the big ones do! Power Take Off Winch (on the boot)... Bumper-Mount trail-skateboard (instead of a heavy-weight trail-bike)... Side mirrors for keepin' an eye out for bears (both the legal types *and* the 4-legged types)... A 120-band CB rig (for tellin' everybody else about the bears)... Fully-equipped kitchen and bathroom - and overhead bed (you'll need 'em all! It'll take *days* to get anywhere with this heavy rig!)... But you won't be bored - just watch the TV (powered by the Onan generator)! *HAPPY HIKING !!!*

TURNING ON THE HEAT

Want to change your campy body odour with some powerful, tenacious smoke smells? Here's your chance! The West Coast Trail usually has fuel in abundance and ideal surroundings for enjoying a fire. While we use a stove for most of our cooking, there are certain times when only real fire can create the true trekking experience. Coffee is big on our list! Our big, stainless steel pot percolates in the coals through and after the dinner hours, providing the best in cowboy coffee. If you catch a cod, or buy some along the way, we think campfire cooking is the only way to go.

Need a reason to invite an interesting person over?
Build a cozy, beckoning fire.

A simple, keyhole fire is the most common for general use. Keyhole refers to the circle of stones open at one end for drawing out cooking coals or setting in a pot. In wind or rough weather, a trench fire will give a more uniform heat for cooking. If you make the trench in sand or beach gravel, you won't need to line it with stones.

FIRE-BUILDING TIPS

• In wet weather, dry wood may be found in the lower dead branches of a large tree, or the inside of a cedar log. Put a good piece of dry cedar under cover for the morning kindling.

• Feed long pieces in from one side of the fire and keep pushing them in as they burn.

• In heavy rain, lean a flat log above the fire to act as a nighttime roof.

• In cold weather, build your fire on the protected side of a big log, which will reflect and radiate the heat. Be careful not to set your fire too close to the log. You may find yourself with enough heat to make bronze, but lose your heat radiator.

• To keep a fire smouldering through the night, roll two six-inch logs side by side over the hot coals and throw on some damp or partially rotten wood. The morning chill may well be avoided.

• Strike-anywhere matches, wrapped in baggies and stored in different parts of your pack, are a smart choice. Don't depend on "waterproof" matches; they may let you down. The most reliable fire starter is a good old Bic lighter.

• Carry fire-starter cubes or sticks. They are light and may save a lot of frustration.

PLEASE DO!

Use a previously developed fire pit.

Use water for extinguishing.

PLEASE DON'T!

Build it near trees or roots.

Leave it burning and unattended.

Leave cans, bottles or other garbage behind in the fireplace.

Place it upwind or too near your tent.

Put your fire out by spreading it around or smothering it with sand.

COMFORT INSURANCE

An extra light-weight tarp always earns its keep!

Use it above your tent in heavy rain.

Sleep under it during clear skies.

When rain persists, rig your fly
up high for cooking or lounging.

Block wind by erecting
a vertical barrier.

Lucky you! Sip your drink in
shade of your tarp

n cold weather, a tarp behind a fire will
reflect the heat.

FOR-WHATEVER-IT'S-WORTH DEPARTMENT

At the beginning of our book, we stated a goal of providing information that would be useful for both the seasoned trekker and the novice. The following tips are offered to all of you, for whatever they are worth.

• Place your feet above your hips when resting on the trail. Your legs will relax faster and you and your toes will become friends again.

• Old film containers make excellent spice containers.

• Place a cap from an aerosol can in the bottom of your tent-pole bag. The poles won't tear the fabric.

• Take care that your tent poles do not become plugged with sand. Partially plugged connections can cause pole tips to break.

• At the end of the day's trek, set up your shelter first. The weather can change very quickly.

• As soon as you get into camp, strip off damp clothes and replace them with dry layers to suit the temperature. This will prevent chills and, in extreme cases, the onset of hypothermia.

• If you are a beachcomber, the best place to find flotsam and jetsam is around the high-tide logs.

• Tie a damp bandana loosely around your neck on hot days. It will act as a radiator to keep you and your photos looking cool.

• Look for hanging clusters of old marker buoys. They signify beach-access points along the trail.

• Wear gaiters, or fold the outside pair of your socks over the top of your boots to help keep sand and blisters out.

• Cut the feet off an old pair of long wool socks. Put them over the top of your boots for instant, recycled gaiters. Looks dumb, but it really works.

• Walking close to the water's edge is often easier than above the high-tide line (the point closest to the trees where you last see seaweed).

• Let a strong hiker set the beach trail first, then walk in her footprints.

• Hike at a pace comfortable for the slowest trekker in your group. This will keep you in sight of each other and help ensure that everyone arrives safely with energy to spare.

• Pita bread and bagels pack well and keep for days. Watch out for crows and varmints, since they like these foods as much as trekkers do.

• When beach walking, beware of any slimy green stuff that grows on the rocks and hard packed sand—it is very slippery when wet.

• When climbing ladders, wait until the person ahead of you reaches a landing. The domino effect of falling trekkers is not a pretty sight.

• Keep your tent well away from creeks and streams. The closer they are, the greater amount of humidity and noise. More important, many of them flood with the tides or the sudden rain showers that frequent the area.

• Keep pack weights well under 30% of your body weight. If you must carry more than this, hire sherpas so you can enjoy the trip.

• Undo hip and chest belts when crossing surge channels and fast-moving streams. This will allow for a quick release should you fall.

• Keep sharp items away from the sides of your pack. It takes very little movement to wear a hole in the material, or in your back.

• A log crossing may appear to be safe, but be cautious. Logs can get very slippery when wet, and they may be tilted at slight angles. Getting injured could literally be as easy as falling off a log.

• Treat blisters with moleskin or second-skin-type products at the first sign of irritation. The added padding on "hot spots" will help prevent a painful situation from getting further out of hand.

• If you get caught on the beach or a shelf with an incoming tide on one side and steep cliffs an the other, head for the points. The points may slope more gently and there may be old access trails or ropes to get you safely back on the trail.

• Keep tent flaps open as wide as possible at night. The fresh air feels great, and the condensation on the inside of your tent walls will be reduced.

• Save your hiking for daylight hours. It is not worth the risk to try and make tide deadlines in the dark.

• Put peanut butter on a squeaky pack connection. It is a good lubricant and may help save your sanity. Be careful to keep your pack out of the way of critters who may be drawn to the smell.

TIDE TABLES

Use of beach routes is often restricted due to high tide levels. Anyone who has experienced the frustration of having to backtrack because of rising tides, or felt the fear of being trapped between steep cliffs and the deep blue sea, will vouch for the value of tide tables.

Tide tables are available free of change at the Parks Canada information centres, located near each trailhead. The tables are for Tofino (a village located on the west coast of Vancouver Island), and one hour must added to the times given to adjust for daylight-saving-time.

The example shown in this section is for a fictional month of July. The table covers a four-day period from Thursday, July 7 to Sunday, July 10. Heights of the tides are shown in feet and metres at their highest and lowest points during the day, as recorded on a 24-hour clock.

EXAMPLE 1:

If you wanted to take the beach route from Thrasher Cove to Owen Point, which is passable at tides below 2.4 metres, on Saturday the 9th, you could do so, starting from 1030 (0930, plus one hour).

Day	Time	Ht/ft	Ht/m
7	0050	3.1	.9
TH	0645	8.5	2.6
	1230	4.3	1.3
	1900	10.9	3.3
8	0155	2.6	.8
FR	0810	8.4	2.6
	1335	5.0	1.5
	1955	10.9	3.3
9	0300	2.2	.7
SA	0930	8.5	2.6
	1440	5.5	1.7
	2050	10.9	3.3
10	0400	1.8	.5
SU	1035	8.8	2.7
	1545	5.7	1.7
	2145	11.0	3.4

EXAMPLE 2:

The beach route between Darling and Tsocowis creeks is passable when tides are below 3.7 metres. During July there are no tides above 3.4 metres, therefore it is safe to trek this section at any time.

EXAMPLE 3:

The surge channel at Adrenaline Creek (known as Adrenaline Surge) is passable at tides below 1.7 metres. On Saturday the 9th, the tide will be at this height at 1540 (1440, plus one hour) and will not go below this depth during the rest of the day. The only time on the 9th that you can go through this dangerous section would be from 0400 to approximately 0700, when the incoming tide is still less than 1.7 metres. We told you to take the trail!

FIT BITS

We have often been asked by potential trail trekkers if we thought they could handle the 75 kilometres length of the West Coast Trail. There is no pat answer. We offer the following comments if you are considering this challenge.

First of all, you must have a positive mindset going into this trip. You can have the strength of Popeye or Olive Oil, but if you are not mentally prepared you will be miserable, you will make others unhappy, and you could get hurt. Bottom line—you have to really want to do this trip!

People have died along this rugged coast. The surge channels are particularly dangerous and the many ladders are not for the faint of heart. Long slippery logs over deep ravines and slimy green stuff at the water's edge are often part of your highway.

You will have to carry a minimum of 30 pounds for at least four hours per day if you expect to complete the trek in six days. Your body needs to be conditioned to handle this amount of stress, so a high level of physical fitness is essential.

Some people make the mistake of going on the West Coast Trail to "get in shape." If you are not physically capable of meeting the challenges before you start, the trail is more likely to injure you than make you more fit. No matter what shape you are in, expect to experience tired, sore muscles at day's end. The good news is, bed never feels as good as after a day of slogging it out in the harness.

SAFE TREKS

The West Coast Trail, in spite of its ruggedness and beauty, can also be hazardous to your health. It does not need to be. Practise safe treks, and reduce the risk. Occasionally, however, matters may be beyond your control. You should be prepared as best you can.

Safest Evacuation Points

Pachena Light	KM 10	Carmanah Light	KM 44
Tsocowis Creek	KM 17	Walbran Creek	KM 53
Tsuquadra Beach	KM 30	Cullite Creek	KM 58
Nitinat Narrows	KM 32	Camper CreeK	KM 62
Clo-oose	KM 34	Thrasher Beach	KM 70

There are about 70 medical evacuations required each year. Most of them relate to sprains, strains and muscle pulls. Wet, slippery conditions, inadequate footwear, poor physical condition, fatigue and excessively heavy packs contributed to these people's downfall. Beware and prepare.

(see A STORY, page 3)

Call 24 hour emergency # (250) 726-3604, or here are some of the people who can help:

- Park Wardens (they coordinate and participate in most search and rescue operations, and perform most of the evacuations)
- Trailhead information centre employees
- Pacheena and Carmanah light station keepers
- Nitinat Narrows ferry operators
- Fishermen off the shelves between Camper Bay and Owen Point
- Coast Guard helicopters
- other hikers (don't be shy if you really need help)

HYPOTHERMIA

Hypothermia accounts for nearly 1 in 10 medical evacuations. It can be fatal if not treated as a life-threatening emergency. It can also be prevented.

Hypothermia results from the body's core temperature dropping to a point where it cannot generate heat on its own.

Uncontrolled shivering is a red flag that hypothermia may be on its way.

Find shelter, build a fire and work hard to dry out and get warm. If the core temperature drops another degree or two, the hiker will become lethargic. The muscles that have been shivering to generate heat will stop doing so. The quality of the person's voice may change. When this happens, there may be a major emergency at hand. Immediate action must be taken to restore body heat. Simply wrapping the person in a sleeping bag is not enough. Remember, the hiker is not generating heat on his own. If possible, strip him and place him in a sleeping bag that has been heated over a fire. Another person, who is also stripped, may have to climb in with him to provide more heat. Do not rub the victim's skin or give him anything to drink when in this condition. In cases of extreme hypothermia, try to locate a park warden to coordinate an evacuation. Once the person's temperature increases, a high-calorie meal will assist recovery.

Remember: Hypothermia can be prevented. We have seen school kids and adults wearing garbage bags in the pouring rain. Better than nothing, but risky. Proper rain gear is essential. Remember to cover your head, as most of your heat loss is through your noggin.

SUN AND HEAT EXPOSURE

If you are lucky, you will be exposed to the sun for extended periods of time. The reflection off the water intensifies the sun's impact, so take care to protect exposed areas of the skin. Bring a hat! Overheating usually happens to a person who is not accustomed to the heat or vigorous exercise.

Victims of heat exertion may became dizzy, suddenly tired, or faint. The best treatment is to rest, cool off and drink extra fluids.

Prevention of heat exertion and more severe heat exhaustion is easy. When you are exercising strenuously in hot weather, you must make a conscious effort to drink LOTS of fluids. For an average person in very hot weather, that may mean drinking four or five litres of fluid a day. **Remember to filter or treat all water**.

FIRST-AID KITS

Every trekker should carry a first-aid kit. It does not have to be expensive, in fact, the home-grown variety may be cheaper and better. Whichever you choose, do not forget to have it handy in your pack.

Suggested items include:
  • Moleskin, or second skin, etc. (for blisters)
  • Band-Aids (wide assortment)
  • Small folding scissors
  • Mercurochrome or iodine
  • Aspirin (also helps keep swelling down)
  • Sunscreen (at least SPF 15)
  • Needle tweezers (slivers abound)
  • Nail clippers (cut them short before you start)
A lot of this stuff can be found on good old Swiss Army knives.

EQUIPMENT

The equipment used on the trail is as varied as the personalities and experience of the trekkers who carry it. We have seen people carrying giant salad bowls, video cameras, and multi-burner stoves. Sleeping bags as big as mattresses and ghetto blasters with giant speakers have all found their way to the trail. At Carmanah, we met one fellow who had all his world belongings on his back. He expected the West Coast Trail to be a road!

Equipment planning breaks down to two choices: blisters or bliss. We prefer bliss.

Unless you have hired sherpas, your pack weight should not exceed 25 to 30% of your body weight. Therefore, a 120 pounds person should not try to carry more than 30 to 35 pounds. A person weighing 180 pounds should draw the line between 45 to 55 pounds unless he plans on beating the heck out of himself!

Rain Gear

The weather along the West Coast Trail is apt to change from fine to foul with little notice. A waterproof pack cover, jacket and pants are mandatory.

Many hikers consider ponchos an excellent means of protection. Ponchos keep most of the rain out, are comparatively inexpensive and pack well. They may be awkward to wear with a pack and difficult to secure in wind. Carrying a pocket-sized one for emergencies is a good idea.

Gore-Tex materials—those that are water resistant but allow moisture out —are very popular. They are also much more expensive than ponchos or their nylon-fabric counterparts. Remember that even these high-tech fabrics are not totally waterproof and can "fail" if you are exposed to rain for too long.

Nylon is a great wind breaker but does not "breathe" well. It works well if you're standing still, but if you are hiking your own sweat will soak you from the inside out. It may be cheaper and pack better than the high-tech fabrics, but it creates sauna conditions when you are working hard.

Boots

Boots are perhaps the most important equipment in your arsenal. Your boots may become your best friend or your dreaded enemy. Choose well —you will be looking at them a lot. The key to good boots is that they must feel comfortable. Yes, there will be a "breaking-in" period after you first buy them. Yes, they will feel better, to a point, the longer you wear them, but DO NOT LEAVE THE STORE UNLESS THEY ARE COMFORTABLE TO BEGIN WITH.

If the clerk tells you that they have to be broken in before they feel good, run—do not walk—from the store.

Boots should be comfortable, lightweight (no full steel shanks) and highly water resistant. Ensure that your heel is held snugly in place. Blisters are guaranteed if your heel rides up the back of your boot, or if your toes are allowed to jam into the ends. Feel the inside of the boot to determine the quality of the finished seams—rough seams equal blisters, smooth seams equal bliss. Soles should be designed with excellent grips (Vibran-type soles are good) and attached to the boot with waterproof seals. A nice touch is for the tongues to be sewn to the sides of the uppers to help keep the elements from leaking in. Firm ankle support is also important, so do not try to do this trail with running shoes. When you are up to your knees in mud around Logan, or climbing the ladders at Sandstone, you will be glad you selected your boots wisely.

Tents

Not everyone hikes with a tent. Some use tarps, one-person bivy sack, or army-issued hoochies. We use a tent with a waterproof fly and strongly recommend that others do too. Whatever you prefer, keep it light and rainproof. Even when it's not raining, the humidity can increase significantly during the night and fog is frequently part of the scene.

Always allow for as much air to circulate inside your tent as possible. We have seen people cover their tents with plastic, or close all their vents when they hit the sack. It's a wonder they survived the night. Maybe they packed oxygen tanks.

82

Stoves

A single burner will serve you well. There are lots of very good styles but we use a Coleman Peak 1 with a 1/3 litre tank. A one-litre Sigg aluminum bottle plus the tank will provide enough fuel for two people if you use it sparingly (no roasting 20 pound turkeys). Add another bottle for every two people. Purists may scoff at using stoves. We have been glad to have them on many rainy occasions and they are environmentally friendly.

Packs

When you are not thinking about your feet, chances are your pack will have captured your attention. Even if there are no outside pockets, you can usually secure whatever you want to your pack with bungies, rope, bootlaces, and just about anything else that you can tie in a knot. There is no great mystery about what type of pack to buy provided you get one that is comfortable. Your pack should have good hip and shoulder straps that are adjustable when you walk. Most of the weight of the pack should be on your hips, so it is most important that the belt is comfortable. The pack adjustment motion, or "West Coast Trail Boogie," will be keeping you busy if your pack does not fit properly. Make sure your salesperson helps you adjust your new pack before you leave the store.

Sleeping Bags

Weight is a key factor to consider when choosing a sleeping bag. Any experienced backpacker knows that every ounce saved adds points to the bliss factor. A three-season bag, which is practical for temperatures down to 0°C, is quite satisfactory. You can always wear your longjohns and socks to bed if you find the chill too much. Synthetic fibres and down bags offer the best warmth/weight ratio.   Synthetic bags are less expensive than their down-filled counterparts. They are preferred for this reason and the fact that they will dry out faster if they become wet. Both types offer excellent comfort within their temperature limits.

Your bag should be carried in a waterproof stuff sack at all times. In addition, we wrap our sleeping bags inside large, plastic garbage bags for added security. At night we put our packs, boots and other miscellaneous gear into the plastic bag to keep critters and humidity out.

Other Equipment To Consider

- This book
- Feminine hygiene products (Monique, of *Chez Monique*, says women ask for these supplies more than any other item)
- Sleeping pad (Therm-a-rests are divine, foam will do)
- Cooking pot (2 to 3 litre), lid is optional
- Tablespoon (no need of forks, table knives)
- Water bottle or camel back
- Matches and/or lighter
- Fire-starter sticks or cubes
- 30 to 50 feet of nylon rope
- Biodegradable soap (use sand for cleaning dishes)
- Toilet tissue (one full roll per person)
- hiking poles (we are latter day believers)
- Warm pants (avoid jeans and other cottons because they soak up water)
- Flashlight (with fresh batteries)

- Wool or polypropylene socks
- Lightweight long johns
- Hat
- Gloves
- Warm wool or polypropylene sweater
- Pile jackets (great if you can fit them in)
- Light weight shoes or sandals (for camp, NOT the trail)
- Nylon waterproof stuff bags (lots)
- Plastic garbage bags (don't forget the ties)

85

FOOD FOR THOUGHT

We have yet to meet a trekker who at some time during the trip did not have his thoughts focused solely on food. The cravings start the first day and build to an obsession by trail's end. The Port Renfrew and Bamfield docks have seated many a blister-footed trekker inhaling cheeseburgers, cold pop and french fries. Some people trek and eat, others eat to trek, but we trek to eat.

Mealtime is a special part of the trip for us. The tent is up, the fire is burning nicely on the beach, and our stomachs are reminding us to get on with it. We stretch mealtime out for as long as we can, restricted only by the degree of our appetites, how much we can pack and creativity of the chef.

Your body will be burning twice as many calories on a trek like this, so it is important to plan your menu carefully. Once you start the trail, there is nothing in the way of food supplies for over 75 kilometres. We have seen people who have been out of supplies with more than a day remaining. This situation could have been prevented with better planning.

Packaging is also important. We still wonder if the bulging plastic bag of pork and beans that one hiker had swinging recklessly from the back of his pack, ever made it to the pot. We wonder too, if the heavy cans of ham and chicken that another had stuffed into her sleeping bag justified the effort needed to haul them up the ladders at Cullite.

Tips:

Hiking the West Coast Trail fosters hearty appetites. We offer the following food tips in good taste:

• Double bag everything. Bag it again in another bag and bag it some more. Take along some extra bags. Rain, heavy dew and unscheduled falls into tidal pools can drench your food supplies and make your trip miserable. Extra bagging will also help prevent spills and leakage into the nether parts of your pack.

• Buy the highest quality food you can afford. Foods containing little or no additives provide a nutritional advantage. Pasta is very versatile, nutritious and an excellent source of carbohydrates. Instead of spaghetti noodles, which are very sharp, try pasta shells. Shells also pack better than bulky macaroni.

• Beginning a meal with hot soup provides a quick, refreshing and easy way to take the edge off your appetite. Your body will be grateful for the fluids. "Mayacamas" brand dehydrated soups are generally excellent. For a hearty meal you can throw in some instant rice and dried peas.

• Japanese ramen soups are light, well packaged and easy to prepare. If you want the taste kicked up a notch or two, try adding a pinch of curry and a teaspoon of crushed chilies. Hang around to enjoy the contorted expressions that follow the first mouthful.

• Garlic, onions and carrots are well worth their bulk and weight since they add a nutritious, tasty touch to your meals. Pack these in a paper bag, or in a manner that allows them to breathe. They will keep longer and you can use the bag as fire starter.

• Keep fuel and stoves separate from the pack that contains the food, unless you like petroleum flavoured fettucini. If you must carry them in the same pack, place the fuel containers lower than the food.

• Hang up all your food at night. The West Coast Trail varmints have been bred to sniff out a package of triple-bagged trail mix at a range of 3 kilometres and they can chew through any pack to get it. Dave's pack looks like a patchwork quilt, yet he is still amazed each time he discovers these critters have gnawed yet another hole to get at their dinner.

EPICUREAN DELIGHTS

Some recipes were created to bring joy and happiness to any trekker. Here are a few we have tried and recommend. The following more or less serve two.

Garlic Pasta

- 1-1 1/2 cups of pasta per person
- 1 bulb (not clove) garlic, chopped
- 1/4 cup olive oil
- 1 handful parmesan cheese
- crushed red chilies or curry powder (optional)

Boil pasta until tender.

Sauce: Heat olive oil, sauté garlic and crushed chilies. Do not brown the garlic, as it will become bitter. Add the sauce to the pasta (do not remove the garlic) and mix in the parmesan cheese. Add curry powder. Serve with plenty of water.   Note: You can add more garlic, at your partner's risk.

Incredible Chili

- 1 cup of vegetarian chili mix
- 1/4 cup of freeze dried black bean flakes
- 1/4 cup of freeze dried mushrooms
- 1/4 cup of sun-dried tomatoes
- 1/8 cup soy mix

Soak mushrooms and tomatoes until plump. Bring three cups of water to a boil.   Add all ingredients and stir well.   Reduce heat and simmer uncovered for 8-10 minutes.   Stir occasionally.   Add more water if needed. Keep tent flaps open at night.

Tortellini Alfredo

- tortellini or shell pasta etc.
- 1 pkg of Alfredo Sauce mix
- handful of parmesan cheese
- pepper and salt
- red wine
- Andrea Bocelli song sheet

If you are camping near a river you may be lucky and find sea asparagus growing below the high tide line. They stand about nine inches above the sand and are green, slender like grass and somewhat gnarly. Steam some of these darlings to really impress your guests.

Boil water (1 part salt to 5 parts fresh adds to the flavour)
Cook pasta.
Add the Alfredo Sauce and stir. How easy is that?
Add optional sea asparagus.
Pour wine!
Sing Andra Bocelli's favourite hits, or not!

Tsk Tsk Couscous

- couscous
- package of precooked bacon, sealed tuna or salmon (these are light weight, tasty and in most grocery stores)
- sundried tomatoes
- package of "tomato, basil sauce mix" or equivalent

Rehydrate tomatoes
Cook couscous
Add tomato, basil sauce mix
Add bits of bacon, tuna or salmon
Sir well and serve hot

French Onion Soup

- package of French Onion soup mix
- cup of croutons or bagel crisps
- two handfuls parmesan cheese
- pita bread

Prepare soup. Add crouton to individual servings and cover with plenty of parmesan cheese.
A red-and-white-checked tablecloth and 1 litre of red wine are optional.

Cowboy Coffee

- 2/3 cup ground coffee (the real stuff)
- 4 to 5 cups of water
- 3 tbsp. honey
- 1/2 cup milk

Boil water in a pan and add coffee. Simmer. Add honey and stir until dissolved. Add milk slowly, stir again and continue to simmer for another 5 minutes. Serve very hot.

Tips:
- Real cowboys may not use honey.

- Scratch a line on your mug at the one-cup mark. This is handy for measuring and essential for making sure your hiking companions don't get more than their fair share of the goodies.

FOOD STUFF

Here are some of the food items we have taken along over the years.

- coffee, tea (herbal and high-test)
- powdered milk
- soya sauce (from your last Chinese meal)
- margarine (butter goes rancid)

- garlic (one of the four major food groups)
- onions
- carrots
- lentils
- couscous

- carob or chocolate bars
- popping corn (it drives other trekkers mad—bring lots)
- trail mix (add lots of M & M's)
- licorice

- Japanese-style ramen soup or Mayacamas soups and sauces
- Taste Adventure Black Bean Chili, or Pinto Beans
- Magic Pantry packaged dinners—heavy but tasty
- Natural High dehydrated meals
- any kind of dehydrated vegetables

- rice
- pasta (all-kinds but spaghetti can be sharp, so watch it)
- instant pancake mix, granola cereal, instant porridge, etc.
- soy burger mix
- olive or canola oil
- brown sugar
- cinnamon
- garlic powder, onion powder, curry powder
- crushed chilies, chili flakes, salsa, etc.
- cheese—parmesan, cheddar, gouda, creamed, etc.
- peanut or almond butter
- crackers—all kinds—lots of uses
- sardines, tuna, salmon, oysters, shrimp, etc.
- dried sausage, pepperoni, jerky, etc.
- pita bread, bagels, etc.
- cookies (make sure they pack well)

LIFE ON THE BEACH
tracking creatures from the intertidal zone

SPLASH ZONE

MIDDLE TIDE ZONE

Beach Hoppers rise around your feet as you walk the sand.

Goose Barnacles collect food as they sway in the surf.

Periwinkles seldom go in the water.

Mussels cling to the rocks by the thousands.

Anemones inject poison into their prey but aren't harmful to humans.

Shore Crabs are purple and green and hide under rocks.

Black Turbans live in tide pools.

LIFE ON THE BEACH
tracking creatures from the intertidal zone

LOW TIDE ZONE

Hermit Crabs live in borrowed snail shells.

Limpets slide over the rocks collecting food.

Black Chitons are protected by overlapping shells.

Tidepool Sculpins, or Bullheads, change their colour to match the surroundings.

TREKKING SOUTH TO NORTH

GORDON RIVER ACCESS

If you are starting your trek from Port Renfrew, the information centre is located at the mouth of the Gordon River, on Pacheedaht First Nation land.

You must get your hiking permit, complete the orientation, receive a copy of tide tables and any last minute instructions. See "Orientation Session" and "Park User and Ferry Fees" (page 12 to 13.)

Be prepared for an exhausting beginning to your trek. As one friend put it: *"Our packs were the heaviest they would be for the entire seven days; our feet were unused to new boots and we had yet to get into the rhythm of the trail. I thought I had started a four -hour walk into hell!"* So much for bliss!

This section has some of the most physically demanding terrain on the whole trail. Recognize this beforehand. Your enjoyment of the journey depends as much on your positive mindset as on your physical conditioning. It bothers us to hear people say, "We had no idea it was so tough!" Take your time! It does get easier. Eventually your pack will become lighter.

Tip:
Whenever possible, lean your pack on a log before putting it on or taking it off. The added height from ground level will save wear and tear on your back.

...AT LEAST IT
AIN'T RAINING...

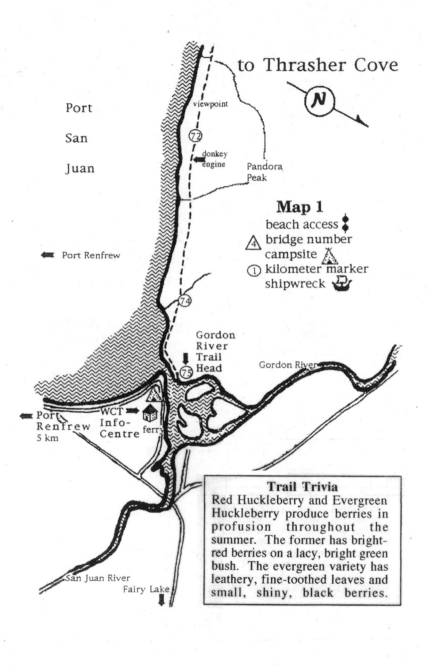

to Thrasher Cove

N

Port

San

Juan

viewpoint

72

donkey
engine

Pandora
Peak

Port Renfrew

Map 1
beach access
△4 bridge number
campsite
① kilometer marker
shipwreck

74

Gordon
River
Trail
Head

Gordon River

75

Port
Renfrew
5 km

WCT
Info-
Centre   ferry

San Juan River

Fairy Lake

Trail Trivia
Red Huckleberry and Evergreen
Huckleberry produce berries in
profusion throughout the
summer. The former has bright-
red berries on a lacy, bright green
bush. The evergreen variety has
leathery, fine-toothed leaves and
small, shiny, black berries.

MAP 1: GORDON RIVER—THRASHER COVE

APPROXIMATE TREKKING TIME: 3 1/2 to 4 1/2 HOURS
DISTANCE: 6 KM

This section is all inland. No beach travel is possible.

The trail starts at sea level at KM 75 and climbs gradually upward for about 3 1/2 kilometre. It crests at the highest point on the trail, a lung-busting 230 metres (about 700 feet.) higher than when you started.

The trail is reasonably well maintained over the entire distance, but a few gullies are bridged with narrow logs. Logs, bridges, gullies and trenches will test the traction of your boot soles. Move with care.

A huge, old donkey engine sits by the trail just past KM 72. We have often wondered at the effort it must have taken for the early loggers to get that machine up there. Hundreds of metres of heavy cable, used decades ago to haul logs to the water, are still stretched taut along the trail. A healthy forest of big trees now blocks views of the water far below.

More steep climbing awaits on the far side of Log Jam Creek (and you thought it was all downhill from here!). The trail undulates until you reach the exit to Thrasher Cove near KM 70.

Some stout-hearted trekkers keep going to Camper Bay rather than face the rugged climb down to Thrasher Cove from the main trail. A few trekkers choose to camp in the woods on top of the ridge on the north side of Log Jam Creek, (about 300 metres south of the Thrasher Cove exit) then continue on to Camper the next day. We recommend that you make the hike to the beach and call it a day.

THRASHER COVE

The side trail to Thrasher is a series of steep switchbacks and ladders that will drop you 50 stories as fast as an elevator. Be particularly careful on this stretch if it has rained recently. The side trail is about one kilometre in length and can be very rough, but it can seem endless on the way back up.

Thrasher Cove campsite is wonderful—lots of fresh water, usually plenty of firewood, a toilet with lovely views (particularly if the window is left open!). Be sure to check out the high-tide line before pitching your tent.

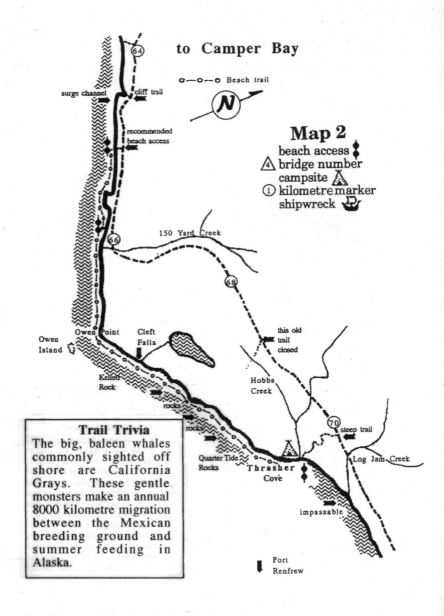

to Camper Bay

○—○—○ Beach trail

Map 2
beach access
△ bridge number
campsite ⛺
① kilometre marker
shipwreck

surge channel
cliff trail
recommended beach access

64

66

68

150 Yard Creek

this old trail closed

Owen Point
Owen Island

Cleft Falls

Hobbs Creek

Kellett Rock

rocks

rocks

70 steep trail

Log Jam Creek

Quarter Tide Rocks

Thrasher Cove

impassable

Port Renfrew

Trail Trivia
The big, baleen whales commonly sighted off shore are California Grays. These gentle monsters make an annual 8000 kilometre migration between the Mexican breeding ground and summer feeding in Alaska.

MAP 2: THRASHER COVE—CAMPER BAY

APPROXIMATE TREKKING TIME: 4 HOURS
DISTANCE: 8 KM

You can take either the beach or the inland trail from Thrasher to KM 65 —tides willing. The beach section offers a variety of hiking terrain, but is more challenging than the inland route. The inland trail is hidden from the ocean for most of the time. It cuts deep into the woods around Owen Point and is an interesting, challenging trek. Be very careful crossing the many logs along this stretch.

Beach Route Option—Thrasher Cove to KM 65

It is important to check tide tables any time you hike the beaches, but it is particularly important for this stretch. The tides must be lower than 2.4 metres to get from Thrasher to KM 65, but remember, they must be below 1.8 metres to get around Owen Point.

The lower the tide, the easier it will be trekking the stretch from Thrasher to Owen Point. The beach is littered with huge crisscrossing logs and enormous boulders. This route may frequently seem impassable, but if the tides are right, and you watch your step, it is a great route to take.

There is a spectacular cave that you must walk through to get around Owen Point provided the tide is below 1.8 metres. If the tide is rising and you find yourself at Owen Point, you may be able to climb over the point rather than taking the cave route. Look for the ropes at either side but don't count on them being there.

There may be sea lions off Owen Point. They can help kill some time if the tides hold you up.

Trail access is available at KM 66 and 65. Both access points lead from the spectacular shelf up to the forest trail. You must take the inland trail between KM 65 and Camper Bay. We recommend you use the access that is located at approximately KM 65. This is the second trail-access marker seen from the shelf north of Owen Point.

SURGE CHANNEL

If you miss the KM 65 trail access, be aware there is a dangerous surge channel between KM 65 and KM 64 that can ruin your day if you try it when the tide is high. The channel can be crossed when tides are below 1.7 metres. If the tide is low enough, a rock will be exposed in the middle of the channel. If necessary, remove your packs and pass them across one at a time. This may not be an easy process, but it may save injury.

The trail access at KM 64 is steep and tricky and should be used by confident, experienced trekkers only. Once again, we strongly urge you to access the trail at KM 65 because of its relative safety.

INLAND TRAIL OPTION

The hike inland from Thrasher to Camper Bay starts with the infamous climb to the main trail from the beach. The elevation is equivalent to a 55 storey building. Once you regain the main trail, for heaven's sake turn left. We have heard of people turning right by mistake!

The trail is well marked. There are numerous boardwalks, planks and fallen trees to carry you from KM 70 to near KM 64. You are never far from the ocean once you reach KM 66. For a change in scenery, you might want to scramble onto the shelf at KM 66 and hike it to KM 65. Make sure the tide is below 2.4 metres. The stretch from KM 65 to Camper Bay can be gooey if it has rained recently, but generally it is a relatively easy trek.

CAMPER BAY

Camper Bay offers excellent, well-protected campsites. There is usually plenty of firewood at the head of the bay, but you may have to do some fancy stone stepping to cross the creek. The creek bed at Camper changes its course every year and sometimes disappears under the gravel before reaching the ocean. Be wary of the tides when you pitch your tent. The creek bed may look innocent, but it floods with the rising tide. We have heard wild blasphemy from trekkers who had snuggled down for the night only to find themselves deep in the brine before their time. Look for the high-tide line and stay above it.

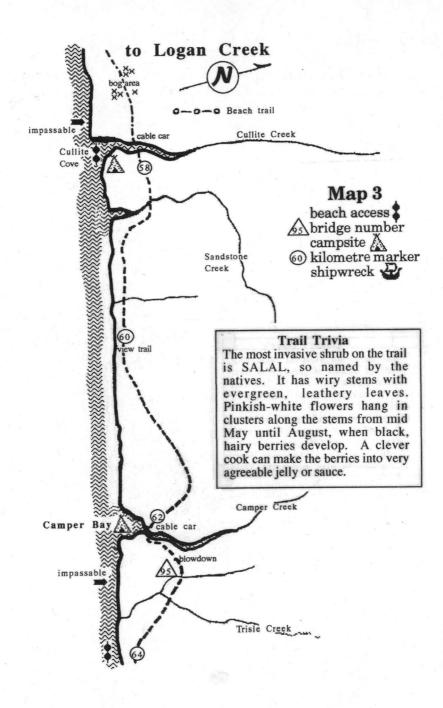

to Logan Creek

N

bog area

o—o—o Beach trail

impassable

cable car   Cullite Creek

Cullite
Cove

58

Map 3

beach access
95 bridge number
campsite
60 kilometre marker
shipwreck

Sandstone
Creek

60
view trail

Trail Trivia
The most invasive shrub on the trail
is SALAL, so named by the
natives. It has wiry stems with
evergreen, leathery leaves.
Pinkish-white flowers hang in
clusters along the stems from mid
May until August, when black,
hairy berries develop. A clever
cook can make the berries into very
agreeable jelly or sauce.

Camper Creek

Camper Bay   62
cable car

blowdown
impassable   95

Trisle Creek

64

MAP 3: CAMPER BAY - LOGAN CREEK

APPROXIMATE TREKKING TIME: 4 HOURS
DISTANCE: 6 KM   (BUT CAN SEEM LIKE DAYS)

They're HEEEEERE! This section includes some of the most challenging, frustrating, muddy and generally interesting terrain along the entire trail. It also has ladders—lots of ladders. Ladders with over 200 rungs (count them), which never seem to end. We are talking ladders that climb the equivalent of a 25 to 30 storey building. Say hello to your cardiovascular system!

This section requires particular attention. Even if it is not raining, the trail can become a quagmire in places, so step with care and be prepared for frequent mud baths. It's great! There's enough mud and goo in this area to coat us all. In a split second you can end up knee deep in the stuff. Should you take the plunge, remind yourself that the world's best spas charge big bucks for this sort of skin treatment. Get your cameras out, the folks back at the office are not going to believe this part of your story.

You will come across your first cable car at Camper Bay. While you may be able to scramble over Camper Creek during the summer season, at other times, high water levels may force you to choose this new found means of transportation.

Cable Car 101
Keep your fingers well away from the wheels!

1) Pull the bottom rope to bring the car toward you.
2) Remove your pack.
3) While a partner holds the car steady, hop into the car and pull in your pack.
4) Grab onto the top rope while your partner steps in.
5) Once all fingers are safe and secure, let go and enjoy the ride.
6) When gravity fails, pull on the bottom rope to reach the platform.

Tips:
We have found that the louder you scream, the faster and farther the cable car goes on its downward run.

Camper Bay to Sandstone Creek

The inland trail is your only option. It is no longer possible to hike the beach from Camper Bay to Sandstone Creek. The route from the mouth of Sandstone to the inland trail is impassable. Even if you were able to bushwack this section, you would find yourself up the creek without a means of getting up the steep, slippery rocks below the trail and the bridge.

The trail climbs sharply when you first leave Camper. While this section may seem easier at the south end, the entire route is a maze of giant roots, minibogs and fallen logs. The forest is glorious. Be sure to pack your sense of humour and adventure.

SANDSTONE CREEK

At Sandstone the ladders seem unending, particularly if you are going up. A bridge across this beautiful creek offers a welcome respite before tackling the ladders on the other side. Once you complete this section of the trail, there will be no beanstalk you cannot scale.

CULLITE CREEK

It is less than 1 kilometre from Sandstone to Cullite Creek. The trail is essentially the same as you have pounded across from Camper Bay. Big ladders greet you at the cable car on Cullite Creek. Sandstone and Logan both have their fair share of ladders, but those at Cullite are the highest of all.

There is a fair, small campsite at Cullite Cove, which is bordered by impassable headlands. You have to go down the creek bed from the trail to get to it.

The trail to Logan moves through a swampy area with boardwalks and interesting flora. Many of the trees are ancient and stunted "bonsai" cousins of giant cedars, spruce and hemlock.

Please stay on the boardwalk along this section to preserve the fragile environment and prevent wet feet.

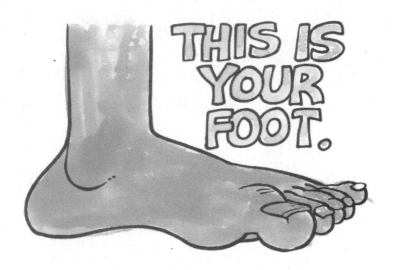

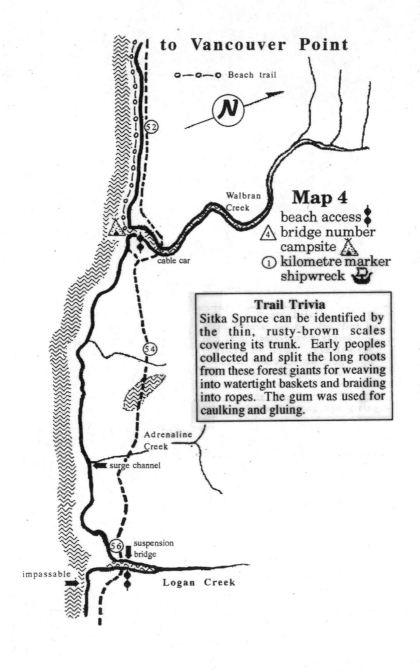

to Vancouver Point

o—o—o Beach trail

N

52

Walbran
Creek

Map 4
beach access
bridge number
4
campsite
① kilometre marker
shipwreck

cable car

Trail Trivia
Sitka Spruce can be identified by
the thin, rusty-brown scales
covering its trunk. Early peoples
collected and split the long roots
from these forest giants for weaving
into watertight baskets and braiding
into ropes. The gum was used for
caulking and gluing.

54

Adrenaline
Creek

surge channel

56 suspension
bridge

impassable

Logan Creek

MAP 4: LOGAN CREEK - VANCOUVER POINT

APPROXIMATE TREKKING TIME: 2 1/2 to 3 hours
DISTANCE: 5 KM

This section has it all: steep ladders, endless mud holes and roots, boardwalks over bog, a dangerous surge channel, a cable car, a wonderful sandy beach, a fabulous swimming hole, a spectacular campsite and a heart-stopping bridge over Logan Creek. What a trek!

LOGAN CREEK

Recent weather events and landslides have destroyed the campsites that were once located at the mouth of the creek. There is no longer access from either end of the trail.

The Logan Creek suspension bridge is a masterpiece of engineering. It offers spectacular, if not heart-stopping, views from its centre. This is the second bridge built over this creek. The first disappeared a few years ago during a major landslide, as did the ladders accessing the beach. The trail here may be hazardous, and the ladders less than perfect. Watch each step carefully through here.

CAMPSITE ADVISOR

Trekkers have often asked us what itinerary we would use if we were hiking the number of days they had allotted. Combine these as you wish and look for more information at **blistersbliss.ca**

Our Preferred, Seven Nights, Eight Days

Day 1: Michigan *or* Darling Creek
Day 3: KM 40 *or* Cribs Creek
Day 5: Walbran *or* Cullite Creek
Day 7: Thrasher Cover

Day 2: Tsusiat Falls
Day 4: Carmanah *or* Bonilla Creek
Day 6: Camper Bay

Six Nights, Seven Days

Michigan *or* Darling Creek
Tsusiat Falls
KM 40 *or* Cribs Creek
Walbran *or* Kulaht Creek
Camper Bay *or* Cullite Creek
Thrasher Cove

Five Nights, Six Days

Darling *or* Orange Juice Creek
Tsusiat Falls *or* KM 40
Cribs *or* Carmanah Creek
Walbran *or* Cullite Creek
Camper Creek *or* Thrasher Cove

If you are planning on completing the trail in less than five nights and six days, you need not our advice, but rather, divine intervention.

WALBRAN CREEK

As you gingerly climb down yet another set of steep ladders, rejoice. The worst of the mud, bogs, roots and ladders is behind you. Walbran Creek campsite is one of the best on the trail. A clear, deep and refreshingly cool (read: ice cold) pond greets weary trekkers. There is plenty of wood for fires and wind shelters. The ocean views are incredible.

The beach is the usual route between Walbran and Vancouver Point. The cable car joins a bypass trail to Vancouver Point and may be the only option if the rains have made the creek mouth impassable. We have witnessed a third of the camping area wash away during a heavy rain. A rock slide, in 2011, blocked the north side of the creek.

"...the beach boogie..."

You may beach boogie between Walbran Creek and Vancouver Point if tides are below 2.7 metres and Walbran is not in flood. We recommend this route. Walbran must be waded when hiking the beach. The water at the mouth is only knee deep during the summer months. It may be much higher during rainy periods. Take care when crossing. If the tide is low enough, walk the shelf—it's flat and hard.

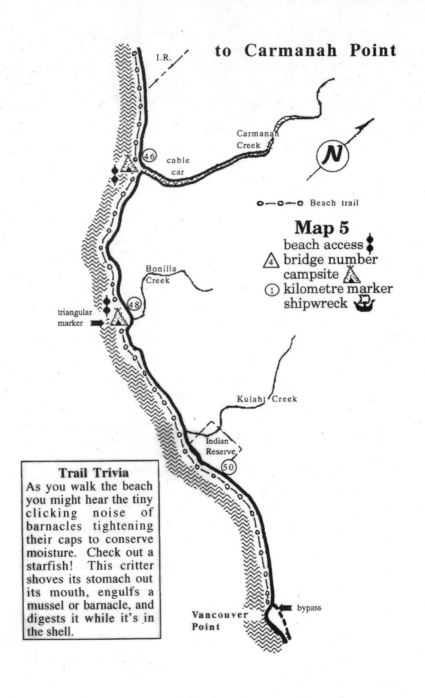

to Carmanah Point

I.R.

Carmanah Creek

46 cable car

Bonilla Creek

triangular marker

48

Kulaht Creek

Indian Reserve

50

Vancouver Point

bypass

o—o—o Beach trail

Map 5
beach access
△ bridge number
4
campsite △
① kilometre marker
shipwreck

Trail Trivia
As you walk the beach you might hear the tiny clicking noise of barnacles tightening their caps to conserve moisture. Check out a starfish! This critter shoves its stomach out its mouth, engulfs a mussel or barnacle, and digests it while it's in the shell.

MAP 5: VANCOUVER POINT—CARMANAH POINT

APPROXIMATE TREKKING TIME: 2 1/2 TO 3 HOURS
DISTANCE: 7 KM

Travel between Vancouver Point and Carmanah Point is all on the beach. There are excellent views along this sandy stretch.

Passage from Vancouver Point to Bonilla Point is possible when tides are below 3.7 metres. There are several pieces of long-lost ships buried here and there in the sand. We have seen several river otters around here. One year we watched a dozen seals herd a school of small fish into the shallows at Kulaht as a prelude to a seafood buffet. Deer occasionally wander by. One actually allowed itself to be scratched behind its ears, just like some trekkers!

...fine sand makes for tough trekking...

BONILLA POINT

Bonilla has a good campsite with plenty of wood and a small waterfall. Look closely at the beach line to the left of the waterfall and you will notice the remains of an old ship (perhaps the barque *Lizzie Marshall* that went down in 1884). Your best option is to hike the beach here, but it is often very tough slogging on fine sand or gravel, as you sink with every step.

This is one stretch where gaiters or spats are handy for keeping the pebbles on the beach and out of your boots. Wayne likes to use the "sand-in-the-boots" trick as an excuse to stop. He takes off his boots, shakes out his socks and enjoys the scenery. It drives Dave crazy!

CARMANAH CREEK

Carmanah Creek can be waded near its mouth during July, August and September. Be careful of the strong current. If you are determined to keep dry, use the cable car. Do not go searching up and down the creek (it is more like a river than a creek) looking for a dry crossing, for they are rare. Park your pack, doff your boots and stroll across near the mouth. Your tootsies will thank you. The beach offers an excellent campsite with plenty of wood, fresh water and postcard-calibre views.

Two kilometres of hard sand beach lead to Carmanah Point and the Light Station. It's a beautiful reward and an easy walk.

Be sure to stop by Chez Monique's near the north end of the beach. Monique (if her settlement is still occupied) will tell you her story about ancient Native claims to the area. Refreshments to satisfy most cravings are available. She also has a shelter for trekkers who run into trouble with the weather.

We know of one soggy person who has benefited from Monique's good will. The first year, he burned his borrowed sleeping bag trying to dry it. The second year, he burned his own tent! We can only hope that for this unfortunate gentleman it will be "third time lucky."

CARMANAH VALLEY TREES

Carmanah Valley is the home of many of the world's tallest Sitka spruce. Some of these giants are over 3 metres in diameter and are estimated to be more than 700 years old. The tallest tree is nearly 32 stories high. We tip our packs to the Heritage Forest Society, Sierra Club and Western Canada Wilderness Committee for their unfaltering efforts to save these treasures from chainsaws.

There is an ancient horn at the Carmanah Point Light Station that no longer blows. It once had the longest series of warning blasts along the coast—three honks every ninety seconds! It could bring tears to the

eyes of weary trekkers who had just tucked in at the end of a long day. Modern technology has rendered the horn obsolete. Today we look forward to the soothing, steady roar of the surf.

CARMANAH POINT

Carmanah Point is crossed either by taking the regular trail and bypassing the light station, or by going through the station grounds. We recommend visiting the station and hiking the beach from there to at least Cribs Creek. There is a long flight of stairs near the helicopter pad that leads to the beach. You are lucky! Many trekkers claim that these stairs are twice as high going up as they are going down! Throughout most of the year there are sea lions off Carmanah Point. You can frequently hear and smell them before you actually see them. Ahhhhhh, the west coast! Our friends, Janet and Jerry Etzkorn, have carefully maintained the Carmanah Light for many years. Stop and admire their garden. You are welcome to walk Janet's homemade labyrinth and get in touch with your inner self.

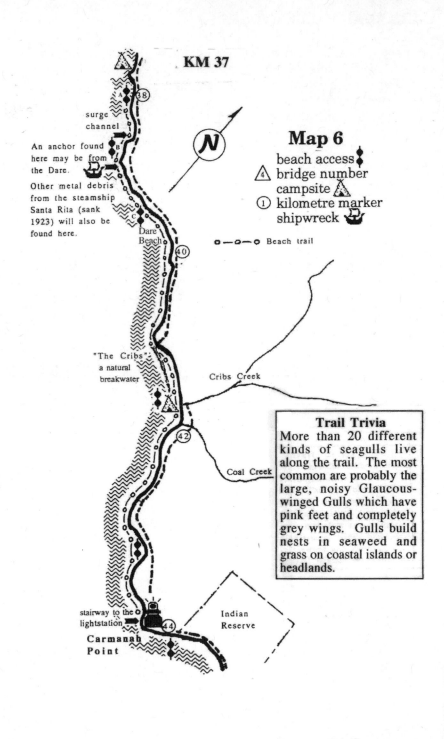

KM 37

surge
channel

An anchor found
here may be from
the Dare.

Other metal debris
from the steamship
Santa Rita (sank
1923) will also be
found here.

Dare
Beach

"The Cribs"
a natural
breakwater

Cribs Creek

Coal Creek

stairway to the
lightstation

Carmanah
Point

Indian
Reserve

Map 6

beach access
△4 bridge number
campsite △
① kilometre marker
shipwreck

o—o—o Beach trail

Trail Trivia
More than 20 different
kinds of seagulls live
along the trail. The most
common are probably the
large, noisy Glaucous-
winged Gulls which have
pink feet and completely
grey wings. Gulls build
nests in seaweed and
grass on coastal islands or
headlands.

MAP 6: CARMANAH POINT - KM 37

APPROXIMATE TREKKING TIME: 2 1/2 TO 3 HOURS
DISTANCE: 6 KM

The stretch between Carmanah Point and the Cribs can be trekked inland or by beach. Either is a good way to go. We prefer the beach, if tides are below 2.1 metres, but the trail route has several interesting views.

CRIBS CREEK

The beach walk from Carmanah Point to Cribs Creek is a favourite of ours. Cribs has a great campsite, with plenty of water and firewood and boasts a natural, rocky breakwater that is a unique coastal feature. It is

easy to hike and the scenery is spectacular.

Thousands of sea birds may be resting on these rocks and along the beach. If you walk through the flock, be prepared for a loud and spectacular show of motion. Wear a hat!

Cribs Creek water is always dependable, so keep your water bottles topped up. Steep cliffs between Cribs Creek and Dare Point block trail access in several places. Be sure of the tide levels and give yourself plenty of time to get through this area.

Do not get caught hiking with water lapping at your feet. Parks Canada recommends that hikers stay on the trail from Cribs to Cheewhat.

There is one other campsite, at KM 40, that may have water. This is a lovely spot and seldom used.

CRIBS CREEK TO KM 37

You can either hike the inland trail from Cribs Creek to KM 37, or take the beach for part of the distance, provided tides are below 2.1 metres. If you take the beach route, we recommend you regain the inland trail at access point B, near KM 39.

There is a difficult surge channel just south of KM 38. If you decide to hike the beach, we recommend that you access the trail near KM 39 and keep on it until KM 37. Look for a steep, short trail that leads up from the shelf at KM 39. This is the preferred route, rather than risking going down from the shelf and eventually facing the surge channel.

The rocks in this area are very slippery. Tides must be below 2.1 metres before you tackle this section. The *Santa Rita*, which went down in 1923, left its debris along this stretch. It can do the same to you. Your safest alternative is to stay on the inland trail.

Tip:
If you insist on going on the beach between KM 39 and Dare Point, look for a grapefruit-sized rock protruding from the north face of the shelf at KM 39. This rock provides the only foothold for getting up or down from the high shelf to the beach. An alternative is to look for a rope that may hanging over the shelf. If it's there it will assist you with your descent. We recommend you take the trail at access point B.

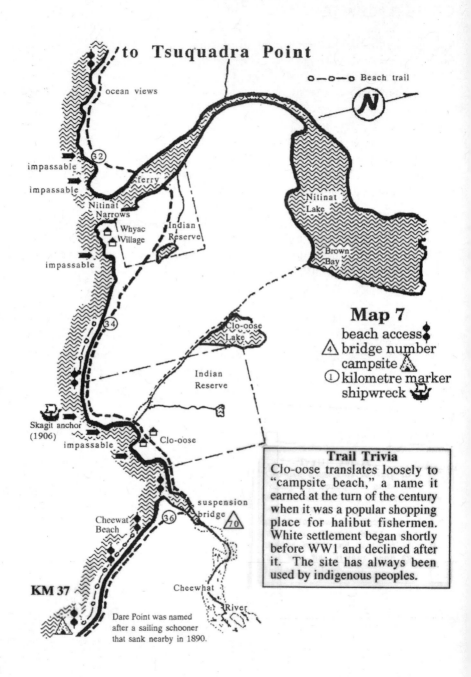

to Tsuquadra Point

Beach trail

ocean views

N

impassable

62

ferry

impassable

Nitinat
Narrows

Nitinat
Lake

Whyac
Village

Indian
Reserve

Brown
Bay

impassable

34

Clo-oose
Lake

Indian
Reserve

Map 7
beach access
bridge number
campsite
kilometre marker
shipwreck

Skagit anchor
(1906)

impassable

Clo-oose

Trail Trivia
Clo-oose translates loosely to "campsite beach," a name it earned at the turn of the century when it was a popular shopping place for halibut fishermen. White settlement began shortly before WW1 and declined after it. The site has always been used by indigenous peoples.

suspension
bridge

70

Cheewat
Beach

36

KM 37

Cheewhat

Dare Point was named
after a sailing schooner
that sank nearby in 1890.

River

MAP 7: KM 37—TSUQUADRA POINT

APPROXIMATE TREKKING TIME: 3 1/2 HOURS
DISTANCE: 8 KM

KM 37
(Time will vary with availability of ferry service at Nitinat Narrows)

The section between KM 37 and Cheewhat is one of our favourites. The woods are peaceful, the trail is very wide and level in most places, and the beach—ahhh the beach!

The good news is that the beach is about 1 1/2 kilometres of lovely white sand. Bathe your blisters and enjoy! Excellent campsites abound. The bad news is that there is almost no water along the entire stretch. There is a small "stream" (read: dribble of water) near KM 37. A pool may have to be dug to get enough water for cooking. Take special care to boil or treat this water before drinking.

While we have camped along this beach many times in the past, restrictions have recently been applied between KM 36 and KM 37 due to an abundance of wildlife in the area. Check with Parks Canada before planning to camp here.

Tip:
If you are staying on the beach and want to get water from the small stream and have trouble getting enough into your bottle, scoop a hole in the stream bed and line it with a few stones. After the silt settles it should make a fine watering hole.

CHEEWHAT RIVER

A funky suspension bridge spans the Cheewhat River. It is user friendly and sometimes provides shade for raccoons and river creatures.

The Cheewhat is aptly named. We have heard that one translation of Cheewhat is "River of Urine"—enough said. If your water supply needs replenishing, look for a small stream off the trail at the North end of the bridge.

WELL, IF YOU'RE OUT OF PERRIER... WE'LL TRY SOME OF THE "CHEEWHAT" MINERAL WATER...

The trail between Cheewhat and Nitinat River has extensive boardwalks that cut across the First Nation Reserve. Excellent time can be made hiking this stretch, but please be careful if the boards are wet. We both have cedar slat imprints on our butts from slips in bygone years.

NITINAT NARROWS

Nitinat Narrows must be crossed by boat. The current runs up to eight knots and the water is cold and deep. The water looks inviting, but it is not drinkable because of the high salt content.

You will be welcomed at the dock by Carl Edgar, Jr., his family, friends and a wonderful assortment of dogs and kids who have lived at this location for many years. They take trekkers across the narrows in their open fishing boat. There may be fresh seafood available here for reasonable prices. Many a year we've cooked fresh lingcod that was so good it brought tears to our eyes! Dungeness crab is another delight to look for. Liquid treats can also be purchased. Please deposit all empty cans in the bins provided.

Timing is critical at this point, since the ferry service operates between 9:00 a.m. and 5:00 p.m. May 1 to September 30. There are several crossings each day, and this is also the departure point for hikers leaving the trail to go to Nitinat Village. Once again, the Nitinat Narrows are always salty. Take care to carry lots of water when you trek this section. Do not rely on getting water here.

TSUQUADRA POINT

The trail rises noticeably between Nitinat Narrows and KM 31. The views are spectacular— even on dreary days. As you leave Nitinat Narrows, the trail dips and heads inland over many boardwalks, bridges, ladders and intertwined roots.

The trail passes through First Nation Reserve near KM 30; and Tsuquadra Point is located in this area. Signs are posted to restrict beach access while in this special area. Please respect their message. Near KM 30 there are some remarkable trees. A bridge that used to cross the creek between Tsuquadra and KM 30 was destroyed in a storm. Take care crossing the rubble.

Beach access is located near KM 29. You can stay on the trail, or hit the sand if the tides are right.

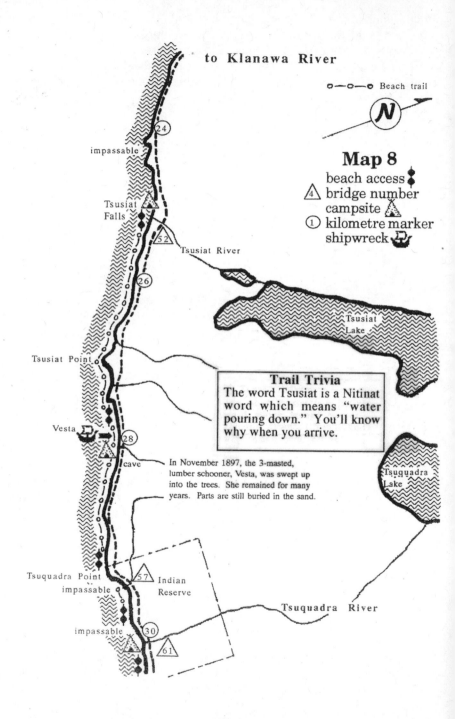

to Klanawa River

○—○—○ Beach trail

N

Map 8
beach access
△ bridge number
campsite △
① kilometre marker
shipwreck

24

impassable

Tsusiat
Falls

52

Tsusiat River

26

Tsusiat
Lake

Tsusiat Point

Trail Trivia
The word Tsusiat is a Nitinat
word which means "water
pouring down." You'll know
why when you arrive.

Vesta

28

cave

Tsuquadra
Lake

In November 1897, the 3-masted,
lumber schooner, Vesta, was swept up
into the trees. She remained for many
years. Parts are still buried in the sand.

Tsuquadra Point
impassable

57 Indian
Reserve

Tsuquadra River

impassable

30

61

MAP 8: TSUQUADRA POINT—KLANAWA RIVER

APPROXIMATE TREKKING TIME: 2 1/2 TO 3 HOURS
DISTANCE: 7 KM

"...a campsite in a cave..."

The route between KM 29 and Tsusiat Falls can be covered either on the beach or via the inland trail. The trail offers periodic views of the ocean. The beach is spectacular, but the sand is loose and can be hard slogging at the end of a long day in the boots.

There is a campsite in a cave along the trail, midway between Tsuquadra and Tsusiat points, near KM 28. The cave, which can serve as a foul-weather shelter, is approximately 100 square metres with enough height for standing. It is noticeable from either direction. Much of the trail is flat here and the trees are magnificent. Beach access trails are identified by the usual array of coloured floats.

Tsusiat Point is passable through the "hole in the wall" if tides are below 2.1 metres. Travel between Tsusiat Point and Tsusiat Falls campsite is an easy beach boogie.

TSUSIAT FALLS

Tsusiat Falls campsite can be reached by beach or trail. It is one of the most popular campsites along the entire route.

Tsusiat Falls is a spectacular natural feature that draws thousands of visitors each year. It provides a refreshing opportunity for sunbathers and dusty travellers to clean up and forget about the rigours of the walk for awhile. There are rock shelves to sit on behind the falls, but be careful— they are slippery and can be dangerous.

The outstanding beauty of this campground is constantly threatened by heavy use. Parks Canada has solved part of the problem by providing a luxurious composting toilet on the north side of the falls. Our role as users is to help keep the sand clean by containing fires and picking up after ourselves. It is no fun having to clean up someone else's mess after sweating it out in the harness all day. We really hope everyone realizes this.

Winter storms and heavy rains alter the campsite dramatically. Sites, which a year ago may have been perfect, might not even exist the following year. Every year is different.

The trail from Tsusiat Falls to Klanawa River is all inland. There are a lot of steady and not-so-steady climbs. Access to the main trail is via some impressive ladders just south of the falls.

"...ladders that seem to never end..."

KLANAWA RIVER

Stay on the trail between Tsusiat Falls and Klanawa River. There are impassable headlands between the beach access at the falls and KM 24. Be extra cautious on the boardwalks here. One bad step could cause grief when you least expect it.

You should take the cable car at Klanawa, as the water is often high, fast and too dangerous to cross otherwise.

If you must wade, keep your hip belts undone on your packs to allow for escape in the event you get dunked. There are campsites by the north side of Klanawa for those who find too much traffic at Tsusiat.

Access to the beach at Klanawa is best gained by continuing on the trail on the north side for a few minutes. The river-edge route is a little more rugged. Branches often extend onto this path and test your good humour.

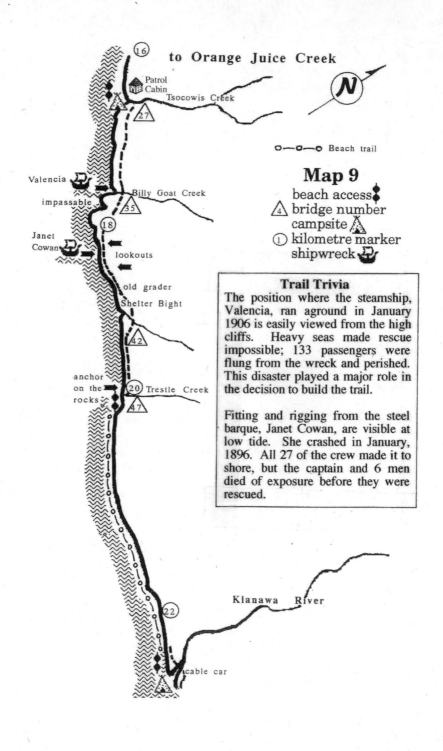

to Orange Juice Creek

Patrol Cabin
Tsocowis Creek

16

27

Beach trail

Map 9
beach access
△4 bridge number
campsite △
① kilometre marker
shipwreck

Valencia

impassable

Billy Goat Creek

35

18

Janet Cowan

lookouts

old grader

Shelter Bight

42

anchor on the rocks

20 Trestle Creek

47

Trail Trivia
The position where the steamship, Valencia, ran aground in January 1906 is easily viewed from the high cliffs. Heavy seas made rescue impossible; 133 passengers were flung from the wreck and perished. This disaster played a major role in the decision to build the trail.

Fitting and rigging from the steel barque, Janet Cowan, are visible at low tide. She crashed in January, 1896. All 27 of the crew made it to shore, but the captain and 6 men died of exposure before they were rescued.

Klanawa River

22

cable car

MAP 9: KLANAWA RIVER—ORANGE JUICE CREEK

APPROXIMATE TREKKING TIME: 2 1/2 HOURS
DISTANCE: 8 KM

The section between Klanawa and KM 21 provides good beach walking, mostly via stone shelf, but with boulders thrown in for good measure.

TRESTLE CREEK

You have to hike the trail from here. Trestle offers a good resting spot. Check out the anchor on the rocks.

The terrain along this stretch varies from easy beach trekking at either end to rugged cliffs with lookouts between Billy Goat and Trestle creeks. Even on the higher stretches, the trail is well maintained and easily hiked. Most of the terrain is flat, albeit high above the water. The inland route between Trestle and Tsocowis is like a stroll to grandma's house.

Look for the old grader on the trail near the Valencia lookout. There is also a rusted-out donkey engine close to Shelter Bight. Early trekkers used to run up and down the trail with these strapped on their backs just to keep in shape, or so the story goes.

VALENCIA LOOKOUT

The views from here are unique and overlook the site where the iron steamship *Valencia* went down in heavy seas in 1906. Out of 160 passengers and crew, 117 were lost. You do not want to be on the beach here under any circumstances.

Tip:
This is a popular place to drop packs and dig into your power bars and trail mix. Be careful where you sit and set your packs. The tree roots at the side of the trail are covered with pitch.

TSOCOWIS CREEK

Steep ladders take you to an excellent campsite next to a waterfall on the north side of Tsocowis. You will find plenty of firewood and water here, and outstanding views from the swinging bridge on the trail above. The lookouts between Billy Goat and Trestle creek provide other opportunities to shoot some frames.

ORANGE JUICE CREEK

The route between Tsocowis and Orange Juice Creek is all on the beach. Orange Juice is a wonderful campsite, with a small waterfall. It is often much more private than some of the more strategically located campsites.

Tips:
When beach walking, beware of any slimy green stuff that grows on the rocks and hard packed sand—it is very slippery when wet.

Do not open the fuel cap while your stove is hot. The contents are under pressure and may ignite when you remove the cap.

To SERVE YOU EVEN BETTER, THE BLISTERS and BLISS CREW IS DEVELOPING AN ONLINE SOURCE OF UNIQUE TREKKING PARAPHERNALIA THAT YOU WON'T FIND IN EVEN THE MOST WELL-STOCKED OUTDOORS STORES! COMING SOON TO THE INTERNET... **B&Bbay** (DOT-SOMETHING OR OTHER)

THE AUTHENTIC-LOOKING™ WALKING POLES

These light-weight units look like you just whittled 'em! Fiberglass with rugged epoxy finish.

$90⁰⁰ EACH
3 FOR $250

AVAILABLE IN:
• BIRCH LOOK
• PINE LOOK
• BAMBOO LOOK
• TEAK LOOK
MIX OR MATCH!

COMING: "WHITE CANE" LOOK

TELESCOPES TO 7½ INCHES FOR E-Z STORAGE!

THE MILES WILL PASS LIKE KILOMETERS WHEN YOU HIKE IN THE

POGO BOOT™

PUT SOME BOUNCE IN YOUR STEP!

INCREASE YOUR STRIDE AN AVERAGE 6.75 FEET!

$150 EACH
3 FOR $425 ☆

BOUNCE UNITS FOLD ALMOST OUT OF SIGHT FOR USE IN CAMP AND WHILE DRIVING.

CARBIDE TIPS AVAILABLE FOR WINTER ICE TREKS.

THE **TAKE A LOAD OFF**™

HELIUM-ASSIST BACK PACK

$275⁰⁰ EACH
2 FOR $600

STOW YOUR STUFF, ZIP THE AIR-TIGHT SEALS, CRANK OPEN THE He TANK, AND FEEL THE POUNDS MELT AWAY.

REFILLABLE HELIUM CANNISTERS AVAILABLE IN "DAY HIKE", "WEEK-ENDER", "MARATHON" AND "COAST-TO-COAST" SIZES.

DOUBLES AS A CAMP-SITE BIRTHDAY BALLOON AND A LIFE RAFT!

OPTIONAL NOVELTY "WHOOPEE-PACK" ADAPTOR: $19⁹⁵

NOTE: SUMMITING MT. EVEREST WITH "TAKE A LOAD OFF" IS NOT RECOGNIZED BY ANY RECORD-KEEPING BODIES

YOU'LL NEVER* MISPLACE YOUR MOST IMPORTANT ACCESSORY... THE

CANADIAN ARMY KNIFE™

GUARANTEED TO INCLUDE TOOLS TO OPEN ANY ALCOHOLIC BEVERAGE CONTAINER KNOWN TO MAN**

*INCLUDES A BUILT-IN GPS AND A STROBE AND A SIREN THAT ACTIVATES IF IT SENSES YOU'VE PUT IT DOWN SOMEWHERE AND FORGOTTEN ABOUT IT!

$199⁹⁵ EACH
(We don't sell more than one per person ~ it's the only one you'll ever need to buy!)

BONUS TOOLS:
• DECORATIVE PAPER PARASOL
• SALT DISPENSER FOR MARGARITAS
• BUTANE LIGHTER
• NAIL CLIPPER THAT CONVERTS TO A ROACH CLIP

**BRUTE FORCE MAY BE REQUIRED AT TIMES

YOU'LL BE THE LIFE OF THE TREK WITH THE

'GATOR GAITER™

$125 EACH
3 PR $370

NO WAY WILL WATER, SAND, PEBBLES OR SCORPION GET INTO YOUR BOOTS* WHEN YOU WEAR THESE... THEY'RE MADE OF REAL ALLIGATOR SKIN!

RUGGED, WATERPROOF, CERTIFIED ORGANIC.

© NELSON DEWEY

HUMANELY TRAPPED & SKINNED SOMEWHERE IN THE THIRD WORLD!

*IN FACT, YOU WON'T EVEN NEED TO WEAR BOOTS, THESE ARE SO TOUGH!

LAST BUT LEAST, THE

INFLAT-A-POTTY™

• PRIVACY AND COMFORT!
• "GO ON THE GO!"™
INFLATES IN 6 TO 120 MINUTES.
(IN FACT, DEPENDING ON YOUR TREKKING DIET, YOU MAY FIND IT BECOMES SELF-INFLATING!)

$79⁰⁰ EACH
3 FOR OH...NEVER MIND.

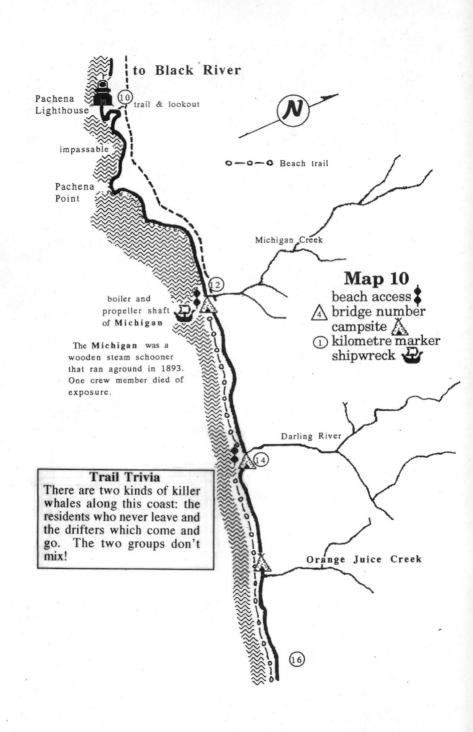

to Black River

Pachena
Lighthouse

(10) trail & lookout

impassable

o—o—o Beach trail

Pachena
Point

Michigan Creek

(12)

boiler and
propeller shaft
of **Michigan**

Map 10
beach access
△ bridge number
campsite △
① kilometre marker
shipwreck

The **Michigan** was a
wooden steam schooner
that ran aground in 1893.
One crew member died of
exposure.

Darling River

(14)

Trail Trivia
There are two kinds of killer
whales along this coast: the
residents who never leave and
the drifters which come and
go. The two groups don't
mix!

Orange Juice Creek

(16)

MAP 10: ORANGE JUICE CREEK—BLACK RIVER

APPROXIMATE TREKKING TIME: 2-3 HOURS
DISTANCE: 7.5 KM

DARLING RIVER

Darling is about 1.5 kilometres from Orange Juice creek, an easy hike on the beach. It has excellent campsites and plenty of water.

Note: There is no trail between Michigan and Darling.

MICHIGAN CREEK

Michigan Creek is about a half-hour beach stroll from Darling River. Michigan has plenty of water, but firewood can be a problem late in the season. This is one of the most heavily used campsites, due to its pleasant, strategic location. There are plenty of campsites on both sides of the creek. The boiler of the *Michigan* which ran aground on the shelf in 1893, is clearly visible at low tide. This is an excellent place to admire sunsets and check out tidal pools on hot, clear days. Whales are frequently seen feeding on the shelf.

PACHENA POINT LIGHT STATION

Pachena Point Light station is about 2 kilometres from Michigan Creek. This stretch is mostly an uphill grade. If the grounds are open there are excellent views to enjoy.

If you are lucky, you will see gray whales "doing their thing" off the rocks at the light station. We have seen them so close to shore that the noise from their blowholes was clearly audible and their spray nearly watered the lawn!

BLACK RIVER

It is an easy 2 kilometres stroll from Pachena Point light station to Black River. Black River is crossed by bridge. The water has a high mineral content, so do not drink it.

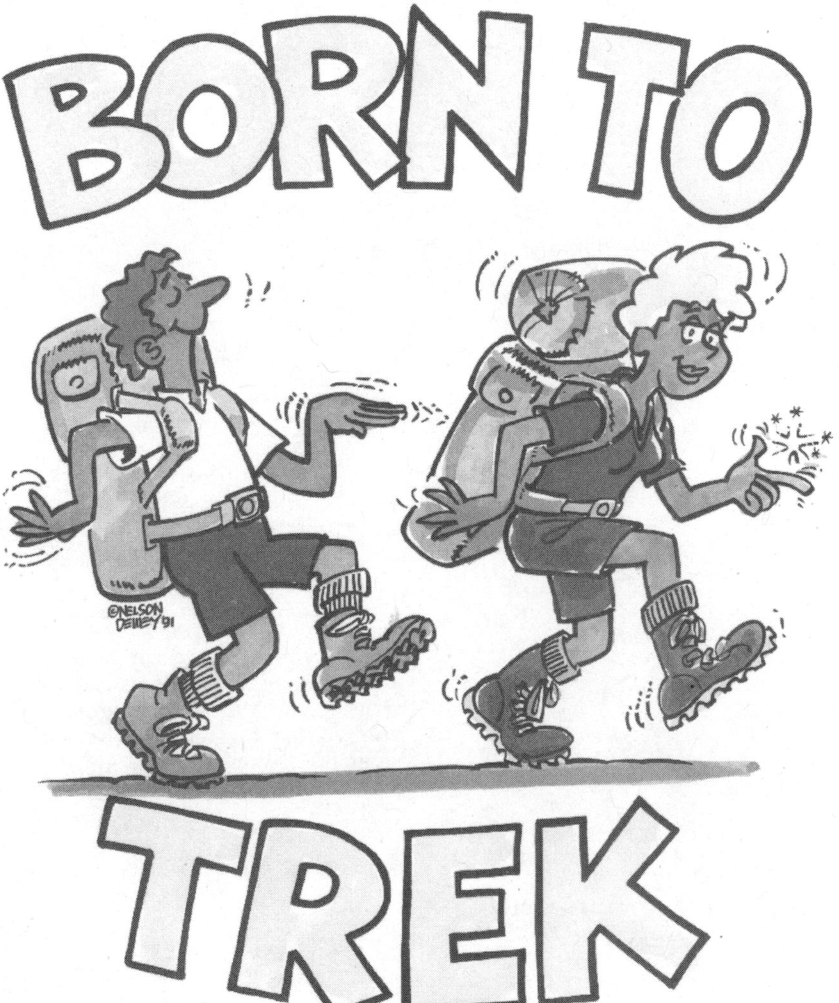
BORN TO
TREK
©NELSON DEWEY '91

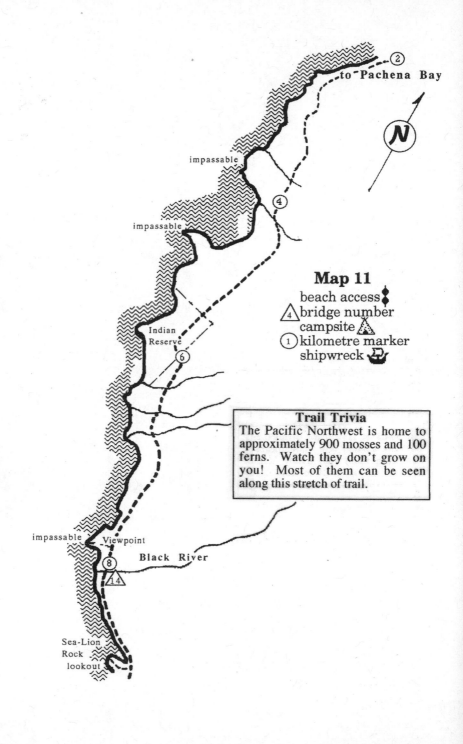

to Pachena Bay

N

impassable

impassable

Map 11
beach access
△ bridge number
campsite △
① kilometre marker
shipwreck

Indian
Reserve

impassable   Viewpoint
Black   River

Sea-Lion
Rock
lookout

MAP 11: BLACK RIVER—PACHENA TRAILHEAD

APPROXIMATE TREKKING TIME: 2 1/2 - 3 HOURS
DISTANCE: 8 KM

There are no fires permitted along the trail between Michigan Creek and Pachena trailhead. The trail is very well groomed along most of this section. It is removed from ocean views and follows high cliffs for the most part, but the woods are wonderful. This is one of the easiest sections of the entire hike. It may provide some welcome relief but do not be lulled into thinking this is an easy stroll. It is 12 km from Pachena Bay to Michigan Creek. Look for a beach access near KM 1 (bridge 4) at Clonard Creek. If tides are below 2.4 metres, you can boogie to the trailhead and bypass the final ladders.

KM 4

Just past KM 4, there is a viewpoint a few meters from the trail. We do not recommend that you go down to the beach at this point. It is too steep for safe climbing. Instead, enjoy the great views here, as well as near KM 6 and KM 8 just north of Black River.

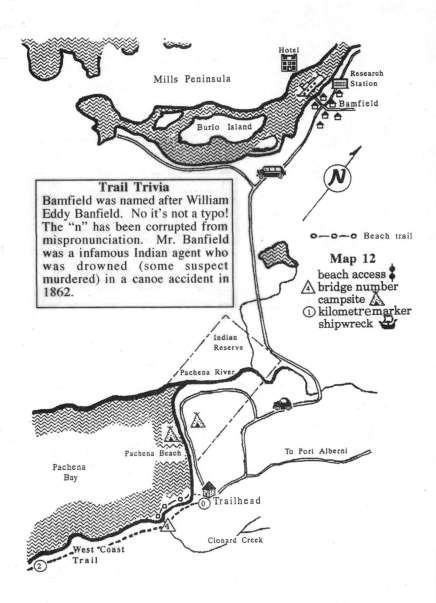

Mills Peninsula

Hotel

Research Station

Bamfield

Burlo Island

Trail Trivia
Bamfield was named after William Eddy Banfield. No it's not a typo! The "n" has been corrupted from mispronunciation. Mr. Banfield was a infamous Indian agent who was drowned (some suspect murdered) in a canoe accident in 1862.

N

o—o—o Beach trail

Map 12
beach access
△ bridge number
campsite △
① kilometre marker
shipwreck

Indian Reserve

Pachena River

Pachena Beach

Pachena Bay

To Port Alberni

Trailhead

Clonard Creek

West Coast Trail

MAP 12: PACHENA BAY—THE END

Congratulations—you made it!

Hikers must sign out and advise the park attendant of any unusual details that could affect those who are just starting.

Depending on your travel arrangements, you may choose to stay on the beach at the trailhead, wait for a bus to take you back to Victoria or Port Renfrew, or take a van that carries you into Bamfield. At any rate, you have just completed a world-class trek, and you deserve to celebrate any way you see fit!

Tip:

It's a long 5 kilometres on a dusty road from the trailhead to Bamfield. Ask the park attendant about the latest transportation information, or check the bulletin board near the parking lot. For a few dollars, it's worth it not to add this stretch to your trek.

"...the road can be hiked..."

TRAVEL CONNECTIONS

Airlines

Victoria and other Vancouver Island destinations are served by:
Air Canada (Air BC), Alaska Airlines (Horizon), Westjet

Ferries

BC Ferries Information...1-888-223-3779
www.bcferries.com
Washington Ferries (out of state) 1-206-464-6400
www.wsdot.wa.gov/ferries/
Black Ball (Victoria-Port Angeles) 250-386-2202
www.cohoferry.com/
Victoria Clipper (Victoria-Seattle) 250-382-8100
www.clippervacations.com
Lady Rose Marine Services... (Bamfield-Alberni)............ 1-800-663-7192
www.ladyrosemarine.com/

Public Transportation

Pacific Coach Lines (Vancouver Island) 1-800-661-1725
www.pacificcoach.com/
Regional Transit (Greater Victoria buses) 250-382-6161
 www.bctransit.com/regions/vic/
WCT Express (Victoria/Port Renfrew/Bamfield) 1-888-999-2288
www.trailbus.com

Other Useful Contacts

Hello BC, West Coast Trail Reservations 1-800-435-5622
www.hellobc.com
Pacific Rim National Park (trail & general park information).250-726-3500
Pachena Bay Information Centre .... Phone / fax 250-728-3234
Gordon River Information Centre .... Phone / fax 250-647-5434
Pachena Bay Campground 250-728-1287
Pacheedaht Campground .... Phone: 250-647-0090

WEBSITES

• Tips 'n Tales of the West Coast Trail
A collection of tips, stories and many links supported by Dave and Wayne.
http://www.members.shaw.ca/blistersbliss/

• West Coast Trail Guidebooks
The official website for ***Blisters and Bliss***
http://www.blistersbliss.ca/

• Pacific Rim National Park Reserve of Canada
Parks Canada has provided comprehensive information to help hikers prepare for the West Coast Trail. We recommend all hikers watch the online videos. Hike safely! There are many tips here, plus a free map and preparation guide.
http://www.pc.gc.ca/pn-np/bc/pacificrim/activ/activ6a.aspx

"... leave only your footprints..."

THE *BLISTERS AND BLISS* TEAM

DAVID FOSTER spends much of his trekking time checking out the flora and impressing others with his skill in building campfires and driftwood furniture. When not chasing critters out of his backpack, David, a retired teacher-librarian, classifies his collection of mosses in his Japanese shade garden.

http://www.blistersbliss.ca

WAYNE AITKEN is frequently seen with his face in campfire smoke, tearfully preparing his culinary delights. His great pleasure is to follow in Dave's footsteps (particularly on sandy beaches). Between treks, Wayne tries desperately to keep his management consulting company afloat.

wtaitken@shaw.ca

NELSON DEWEY is an acclaimed cartoonist and illustrator. His work has appeared in numerous national magazines. He has illustrated over 30 outdoors and "how-to" books.

http://nelsondewey.com/